ALL IN THE TIMING

DAVID IVES

ALL IN THE TIMING

David Ives was born in Chicago and educated at Northwestern
University and the Yale School of Drama. He won the 1994
Outer Critics Circle John Gassner Playwriting Award for the
Primary Stages production of *All in the Timing,* which was also
nominated for a Drama Desk Award as Outstanding Play. He is
the author as well of an opera and short stories, and he has written for Hollywood and television. He lives in New York City.

ALL IN THE TIMING

ALL IN THE

TIMING

FOURTEEN PLAYS

DAVID IVES

VINTAGE BOOKS

A DIVISION OF RANDOM HOUSE, INC.

NEW YORK

A VINTAGE ORIGINAL, JANUARY 1995
First Edition

Copyright © 1989, 1990, 1992, 1994 by David Ives

Library of Congress Cataloging-in-Publication Data
Ives, David.
All in the timing : fourteen plays / David Ives.—1st
Vintage ed., 1st ed.
p. cm.
ISBN 0-679-75928-X
I. Title.
PS3559.V435A82   1995
812'.54—dc20   94-27357
CIP

Book design by Debbie Glasserman

Manufactured in the United States of America
10 9 8 7 6 5 4

CONTENTS

PREFACE

Thank you for your very kind letter about my plays. Here are the answers to your questions:

1. Longhand, with Bic blue medium-point pens.

2. Mornings from 9:00 till lunch, and again in the evenings if I'm really onto something. *Sure Thing* got written in two successive nights between about 11:00 P.M. and 3 A.M. (and then, of course, much *re*written in rehearsal). *Long Ago and Far Away* took months.

3. The South Side of Chicago.

4. Yes.

5. No.

6. "Pinocchio."

7. Absolutely not.

8. My aunt Jo.

9. I was about nine or ten. I found an antiquated, bloody thriller called *Mr. Strang* on my parents' bookshelves and turned its three hundred pages of mayhem into a headlong fifteen-minute play. (Obviously the short form attracted me from a tender age.) What I didn't know at age ten was that everybody in the cast had to get a copy of the script, so after learning my lines I passed my handwritten pages on to Johnny Stanislawski down the block, and he lost them. Probably my greatest work.

10. Ironically, my first date was with a girl whose last name was Kafka, and I took her to see *The Sound of Music*. God knows how that experience warped me, but several therapists have turned me down for treatment on the basis of it.

11. Anchovies.

12. By moistening the tip and saying, "Wankel Rotary Engine," of course.

13. I think Father Henkel did it. He was my English teacher in the rather peculiar, old-fashioned high school I attended (Catholic, all boys, jackets and ties, four years of Latin, the works). One particular afternoon Henkel was trying to focus our young attentions on Emily Dickinson. Unfortunately for Henkel (and Emily Dickinson) it was a warm spring day and we boys were feeling, well, boisterous. Faced with chaos, he laid the textbook down, climbed up onto his desk, and stood on his head. We all stopped horsing around and stared at him in stupefaction. Henkel then climbed back down, picked up the book, and said, "Let's get back to 'Beauty be not caused—it is,' page 388." It was probably my first glimpse of the power of the theatrical: you gather an audience, you do a headstand to get everyone's attention, and then you're free to explore beauty, poetry, truth, the human condition, what you will. Now *that's* an education.

14. No, I never have. Too messy.

15. It happened right around the same time as Henkel's headstand. I was about sixteen and had bought a balcony ticket to see a matinee of *A Delicate Balance* with Hume Cronyn and Jessica Tandy. I remember sitting in the balcony that afternoon watching Hume Cronyn do the speech about the cat (in my memory, I'm sitting in the first row of the balcony staring down at the stage as if I were in the first car of a roller coaster) and thinking that there couldn't be anyplace in the world more thrilling than where I was right then. Maybe the height just made me dizzy. Anyway, that day I started writing plays in earnest, so by the time I reached college I was already in my fertile middle period.

16. Frankly, I don't think it's any of your business.

17. When I was twenty-one, a grant got me my first professional production in a remote area of Los Angeles at America's smallest, and possibly worst theater, in a storefront that had a pillar dead center in the middle of the stage. That play was called *Canvas,* and it catapulted me into immediate and total obscurity.

18. Panty hose.

19. Very often. In fact during my twenties I left the theater not once but twice—only to come back when I realized that nobody knew I'd left. (What are you leaving, when you "leave" the theater? It's the kind of question a Buddhist monk answers by hitting you on the head with a plank.)

20. Probably the production in which the actress playing the lead made her entrance on opening night and the door came off the hinges. I walked out at intermission and came back three years later.

21. (a) Yale Drama School, and (b) not really, what with the head of the playwriting department busy digging trenches outside the cherry orchard trying to keep Sam Shepard out. Yale was a blissful time for me, in spite of the fact that there is slush on the ground in New Haven 238 days a year.

22. The Manhattan Punch Line Theatre, on West Forty-second Street. Much reviled then, much missed now, the Punch Line went bankrupt several years ago. Steve Kaplan, God bless him, ran it with an air of inimitable, hopeless gloom, and always found a place in his annual one-act festival for one or more of my pieces. Unpaid interns, an asthmatic Xerox machine, seething actors—it was real theater. The kind of place where the shows have to be good, because the bathrooms aren't working.

23. Yes.

24. Yes.

25. Yes I said yes I will Yes.

26. *All in the Timing* was the collective title for the Primary Stages production of *Sure Thing, Words, Words, Words, The Universal Language, Philip Glass Buys a Loaf of Bread, The Philadelphia*, and *Variations on the Death of Trotsky*. It was directed by the brilliant Jason McConnell Buzas, who also directed the premieres of several other of these plays and whose stamp (a rare Polynesian first-class airmail) is on practically every one.

27. Mrs. Peacock, in the library, with the lead pipe.

28. The great crested orc.

29. Did you mean "bunion" or "onion"? The difference is, of course, crucial.

30. *Variations on the Death of Trotsky* was not originally intended for production. I wrote it as a birthday gift for Fred Sanders, who directed the first production of *Words, Words, Words*. I had seen an article in the *Times* about Trotsky which mentioned that after being hit in the head with a mountain-climber's axe, Trotsky lived on for thirty-six hours. I thought it was the funniest thing I'd ever heard, and I got very taken with the question of what one does for thirty-six hours with a mountain-climber's axe in one's head. What kind of food do you eat? (Fast food, naturally.)

31. *Mere Mortals* was inspired by an article in a New Jersey newspaper about a guy in an old-folks home who was trying to claim the Lindbergh baby's inheritance. I originally intended to call the play "Perkin Warbeck," but a rioting mob stopped me.

32. *The Philadelphia* was my affectionate revenge on the City of Brotherly Love after I'd spent many miserable months there working on an opera commission and finding myself up against that town's peculiar metaphysical, ah, peculiarities. Bakeries that didn't have any bread on the shelves, for example. Magazine stands that didn't sell *Time* magazine. Or the morning when I tried to get a cheese omelette for breakfast at a restaurant.

> Me: I'll have a cheese omelette, please.
> Waitress: Sure, what kinda cheese you want?
> Me: What kind do you have?
> Waitress: Any kinda cheese. You name it.
> Me: Okay. I'll have Swiss.
> Waitress: Sorry. We don't have any Swiss.
> Me: Oh. Cheddar, then.
> Waitress: No cheddar.
> Me: Monterey jack?
> Waitress: Just ran out.
> Me: Jarlsberg . . . ?
> Waitress: What's that?

33. Yes, *Sure Thing* was written several years before the movie *Groundhog Day*, which bears it a superficial resemblance.

Originally I planned to set the play at a bus stop, and I wanted to write something that would trace all the possible routes the answer to a simple question could take. As for *Foreplay,* I was overdosing on Glenn Gould's recording of *The Well-Tempered Clavier* and had an idea for a play that worked like a fugue. Originally it was to be four secretaries at four desks with four telephones, but somehow a miniature-golf course suggested itself as richer ground.

34. Love. What else?

35. Oop scoopa wee-bop, bonk, *deek!*

36. *The Universal Language* started life as a twenty-minute opera for three singers as part of a commission in dreaded Philadelphia. (Jarlsberg? What's that?) I had long wanted to try writing a play in a language I myself made up, so the composer and I wrote several scenes and presented it in front of an audience as a work in progress. Somehow the piece didn't work, though it was interesting enough. Years later I realized that it hadn't worked because the music was redundant. Unamunda, the made-up language, *was* the music. I took the basic idea, the names of Don and Dawn, and started from scratch, with better results.

37. Does it ever strike you that life is like a list of answers, in which you have to glean or even make up the questions yourself? Just asking.

38. Two reams of paper, several bottles of Jim Beam, and a seemingly indestructible copy of Bizet's *The Pearl Fishers.*

39. Martha Stoberock, who keeps me reminded that the really important things in life don't have anything to do with the theater.

40. Lithuanian chutney.

41. Panty hose.

Sincerely,
DAVID IVES
JUNE 1994

ALL IN THE TIMING

SURE
THING

*This play is for
Jason Buzas*

Sure Thing was first presented at the Manhattan Punch Line Theatre (Steve Kaplan, artistic director) in New York City in February 1988. It was directed by Jason McConnell Buzas; the set design was by Stanley A. Meyer; costume design was by Michael S. Schler; lighting design was by Joseph R. Morley. The cast was as follows:

BILL   Robert Stanton
BETTY   Nancy Opel

BETTY, *a woman in her late twenties, is reading at a café table. An empty chair is opposite her.* BILL, *same age, enters.*

BILL: Excuse me. Is this chair taken?

BETTY: Excuse me?

BILL: Is this taken?

BETTY: Yes it is.

BILL: Oh. Sorry.

BETTY: Sure thing.

(*A bell rings softly.*)

BILL: Excuse me. Is this chair taken?

BETTY: Excuse me?

BILL: Is this taken?

BETTY: No, but I'm expecting somebody in a minute.

BILL: Oh. Thanks anyway.

BETTY: Sure thing.

(*A bell rings softly.*)

BILL: Excuse me. Is this chair taken?

BETTY: No, but I'm expecting somebody very shortly.

BILL: Would you mind if I sit here till he or she or it comes?

BETTY (*glances at her watch*): They do seem to be pretty late. . . .

BILL: You never know who you might be turning down.

BETTY: Sorry. Nice try, though.

BILL: Sure thing.

(*Bell.*)

Is this seat taken?

BETTY: No it's not.

BILL: Would you mind if I sit here?

BETTY: Yes I would.

BILL: Oh.

(*Bell.*)

Is this chair taken?

BETTY: No it's not.

BILL: Would you mind if I sit here?

BETTY: No. Go ahead.

BILL: Thanks. (*He sits. She continues reading.*) Everyplace else seems to be taken.

BETTY: Mm-hm.

BILL: Great place.

BETTY: Mm-hm.

BILL: What's the book?

BETTY: I just wanted to read in quiet, if you don't mind.

BILL: No. Sure thing.

(*Bell.*)

BILL: Everyplace else seems to be taken.

BETTY: Mm-hm.

BILL: Great place for reading.

BETTY: Yes, I like it.

BILL: What's the book?

BETTY: *The Sound and the Fury.*

BILL: Oh. Hemingway.

(*Bell.*)

What's the book?

BETTY: *The Sound and the Fury.*

BILL: Oh. Faulkner.

BETTY: Have you read it?

BILL: Not . . . actually. I've sure read *about* it, though. It's supposed to be great.

BETTY: It is great.

BILL: I hear it's great. (*Small pause.*) Waiter?

(*Bell.*)

What's the book?

BETTY: *The Sound and the Fury.*

BILL: Oh. Faulkner.

BETTY: Have you read it?

BILL: I'm a Mets fan, myself.

(*Bell.*)

BETTY: Have you read it?

BILL: Yeah, I read it in college.

BETTY: Where was college?

BILL: I went to Oral Roberts University.

(*Bell.*)

BETTY: Where was college?

BILL: I was lying. I never really went to college. I just like to party.

(*Bell.*)

BETTY: Where was college?

BILL: Harvard.

BETTY: Do you like Faulkner?

BILL: I love Faulkner. I spent a whole winter reading him once.

BETTY: I've just started.

BILL: I was so excited after ten pages that I went out and bought everything else he wrote. One of the greatest reading experiences of my life. I mean, all that incredible psychological understanding. Page after page of gorgeous prose. His profound grasp of the mystery of time and human existence. The smells of the earth . . . What do you think?

BETTY: I think it's pretty boring.

(*Bell.*)

BILL: What's the book?

BETTY: *The Sound and the Fury.*

BILL: Oh! Faulkner!

BETTY: Do you like Faulkner?

BILL: I love Faulkner.

BETTY: He's incredible.

BILL: I spent a whole winter reading him once.

BETTY: I was so excited after ten pages that I went out and bought everything else he wrote.

BILL: All that incredible psychological understanding.

BETTY: And the prose is so gorgeous.

BILL: And the way he's grasped the mystery of time—

BETTY: —and human existence. I can't believe I've waited this long to read him.

BILL: You never know. You might not have liked him before.

BETTY: That's true.

BILL: You might not have been ready for him. You have to hit these things at the right moment or it's no good.

BETTY: That's happened to me.

BILL: It's all in the timing. (*Small pause.*) My name's Bill, by the way.

BETTY: I'm Betty.

BILL: Hi.

BETTY: Hi. (*Small pause.*)

BILL: Yes I thought reading Faulkner was . . . a great experience.

BETTY: Yes. (*Small pause.*)

BILL: *The Sound and the Fury* . . . (*Another small pause.*)

BETTY: Well. Onwards and upwards. (*She goes back to her book.*)

BILL: Waiter—?

(*Bell.*)

You have to hit these things at the right moment or it's no good.

BETTY: That's happened to me.

BILL: It's all in the timing. My name's Bill, by the way.

BETTY: I'm Betty.

BILL: Hi.

BETTY: Hi.

BILL: Do you come in here a lot?

BETTY: Actually I'm just in town for two days from Pakistan.

BILL: Oh. Pakistan.

(*Bell.*)

My name's Bill, by the way.

BETTY: I'm Betty.

BILL: Hi.

BETTY: Hi.

BILL: Do you come in here a lot?

BETTY: Every once in a while. Do you?

BILL: Not so much anymore. Not as much as I used to. Before my nervous breakdown.

(*Bell.*)

Do you come in here a lot?

BETTY: Why are you asking?

BILL: Just interested.

BETTY: Are you really interested, or do you just want to pick me up?

BILL: No, I'm really interested.

BETTY: Why would you be interested in whether I come in here a lot?

BILL: I'm just . . . getting acquainted.

BETTY: Maybe you're only interested for the sake of making small talk long enough to ask me back to your place to listen to some music, or because you've just rented this great tape for your VCR, or because you've got some terrific unknown Django Reinhardt record, only all you really want to do is fuck—which you won't do very well—after which you'll go into the bathroom and pee very loudly, then pad into the kitchen and get yourself a beer from the refrigerator without asking me whether I'd like anything, and then you'll proceed to lie back down beside and confess that you've got a girlfriend named Stephanie who's away at medical school in Belgium for a year, and that you've been involved with her—*off and on*—in what you'll call a very "intricate" relationship, for the past *seven YEARS*. None of which *interests* me, mister!

BILL: Okay.

(*Bell.*)

Do you come in here a lot?

BETTY: Every other day, I think.

BILL: I come in here quite a lot and I don't remember seeing you.

BETTY: I guess we must be on different schedules.

BILL: Missed connections.

BETTY: Yes. Different time zones.

BILL: Amazing how you can live right next door to somebody in this town and never even know it.

BETTY: I know.

BILL: City life.

BETTY: It's crazy.

BILL: We probably pass each other in the street every day. Right in front of this place, probably.

BETTY: Yep.

BILL (*looks around*): Well the waiters here sure seem to be in some different time zone. I can't seem to locate one anywhere. . . . Waiter! (*He looks back.*) So what do you— (*He sees that she's gone back to her book.*)

BETTY: I beg pardon?

BILL: Nothing. Sorry.

(*Bell.*)

BETTY: I guess we must be on different schedules.

BILL: Missed connections.

BETTY: Yes. Different time zones.

BILL: Amazing how you can live right next door to somebody in this town and never even know it.

BETTY: I know.

BILL: City life.

BETTY: It's crazy.

BILL: You weren't waiting for somebody when I came in, were you?

BETTY: Actually I was.

BILL: Oh. Boyfriend?

BETTY: Sort of.

BILL: What's a sort-of boyfriend?

BETTY: My husband.

BILL: Ah-ha.

(*Bell.*)

You weren't waiting for somebody when I came in, were you?

BETTY: Actually I was.

BILL: Oh. Boyfriend?

BETTY: Sort of.

BILL: What's a sort-of boyfriend?

BETTY: We were meeting here to break up.

BILL: Mm-hm . . .

(*Bell.*)

What's a sort-of boyfriend?

BETTY: My lover. Here she comes right now!

(*Bell.*)

BILL: You weren't waiting for somebody when I came in, were you?

BETTY: No, just reading.

BILL: Sort of a sad occupation for a Friday night, isn't it? Reading here, all by yourself?

BETTY: Do you think so?

BILL: Well sure. I mean, what's a good-looking woman like you doing out alone on a Friday night?

BETTY: Trying to keep away from lines like that.

BILL: No, listen—

(*Bell.*)

You weren't waiting for somebody when I came in, were you?

BETTY: No, just reading.

BILL: Sort of a sad occupation for a Friday night, isn't it? Reading here all by yourself?

BETTY: I guess it is, in a way.

BILL: What's a good-looking woman like you doing out alone on a Friday night anyway? No offense, but . . .

BETTY: I'm out alone on a Friday night for the first time in a very long time.

BILL: Oh.

BETTY: You see, I just recently ended a relationship.

BILL: Oh.

BETTY: Of rather long standing.

BILL: I'm sorry. (*Small pause.*) Well listen, since reading by yourself *is* such a sad occupation for a Friday night, would you like to go elsewhere?

BETTY: No . . .

BILL: Do something else?

BETTY: No thanks.

BILL: I was headed out to the movies in a while anyway.

BETTY: I don't think so.

BILL: Big chance to let Faulkner catch his breath. All those long sentences get him pretty tired.

BETTY: Thanks anyway.

BILL: Okay.

BETTY: I appreciate the invitation.

BILL: Sure thing.

(*Bell.*)

You weren't waiting for somebody when I came in, were you?

BETTY: No, just reading.

BILL: Sort of a sad occupation for a Friday night, isn't it? Reading here all by yourself?

BETTY: I guess I was trying to think of it as existentially romantic. You know—cappuccino, great literature, rainy night . . .

BILL: That only works in Paris. We *could* hop the late plane to Paris. Get on a Concorde. Find a café . . .

BETTY: I'm a little short on plane fare tonight.

BILL: Darn it, so am I.

BETTY: To tell you the truth, I was headed to the movies after I finished this section. Would you like to come along? Since you can't locate a waiter?

BILL: That's a very nice offer, but . . .

BETTY: Uh-huh. Girlfriend?

BILL: Two, actually. One of them's pregnant, and Stephanie—

(*Bell.*)

BETTY: Girlfriend?

BILL: No, I don't have a girlfriend. Not if you mean the castrating bitch I dumped last night.

(*Bell.*)

BETTY: Girlfriend?

BILL: Sort of. Sort of.

BETTY: What's a sort-of girlfriend?

BILL: My mother.

(*Bell.*)

    I just ended a relationship, actually.

BETTY: Oh.

BILL: Of rather long standing.

BETTY: I'm sorry to hear it.

BILL: This is my first night out alone in a long time. I feel a little bit at sea, to tell you the truth.

BETTY: So you didn't stop to talk because you're a Moonie, or you have some weird political affiliation—?

BILL: Nope. Straight-down-the-ticket Republican.

(*Bell.*)

Straight-down-the-ticket Democrat.

(*Bell.*)

Can I tell you something about politics?

(*Bell.*)

I like to think of myself as a citizen of the universe.

(*Bell.*)

I'm unaffiliated.

BETTY: That's a relief. So am I.

BILL: I vote my beliefs.

BETTY: Labels are not important.

BILL: Labels are not important, exactly. Take me, for example. I mean, what does it matter if I had a two-point at—

(*Bell.*)

three-point at—

(*Bell.*)

four-point at college? Or if I did come from Pittsburgh—

(*Bell.*)

Cleveland—

(*Bell.*)

Westchester County?

BETTY: Sure.

BILL: I believe that a man is what he is.

(*Bell.*)

A person is what he is.

(*Bell.*)

A person is . . . what they are.

BETTY: I think so too.

BILL: So what if I admire Trotsky?

(*Bell.*)

So what if I once had a total-body liposuction?

(*Bell.*)

So what if I don't have a penis?

(*Bell.*)

So what if I spent a year in the Peace Corps? I was acting on my convictions.

BETTY: Sure.

BILL: You just can't hang a sign on a person.

BETTY: Absolutely. I'll bet you're a Scorpio.

(*Many bells ring.*)

Listen, I was headed to the movies after I finished this section. Would you like to come along?

BILL: That sounds like fun. What's playing?

BETTY: A couple of the really early Woody Allen movies.

BILL: Oh.

BETTY: You don't like Woody Allen?

BILL: Sure. I like Woody Allen.

BETTY: But you're not crazy about Woody Allen.

BILL: Those early ones kind of get on my nerves.

BETTY: Uh-huh.

(*Bell.*)

BILL: Y'know I was headed to the—

BETTY (*simultaneously*): I was thinking about—

BILL: I'm sorry.

BETTY: No, go ahead.

BILL: I was going to say that I was headed to the movies in a little while, and . . .

BETTY: So was I.

BILL: The Woody Allen festival?

BETTY: Just up the street.

BILL: Do you like the early ones?

BETTY: I think anybody who doesn't ought to be run off the planet.

BILL: How many times have you seen *Bananas*?

BETTY: Eight times.

BILL: Twelve. So are you still interested? (*Long pause.*)

BETTY: Do you like Entenmann's crumb cake . . . ?

BILL: Last night I went out at two in the morning to get one. Did you have an Etch-a-Sketch as a child?

BETTY: Yes! And do you like Brussels sprouts? (*Pause.*)

BILL: No, I think they're disgusting.

BETTY: They *are* disgusting!

BILL: Do you still believe in marriage in spite of current sentiments against it?

BETTY: Yes.

BILL: And children?

BETTY: Three of them.

BILL: Two girls and a boy.

BETTY: Harvard, Vassar, and Brown.

BILL: And will you love me?

BETTY: Yes.

BILL: And cherish me forever?

BETTY: Yes.

BILL: Do you still want to go to the movies?

BETTY: Sure thing.

BILL AND BETTY (*together*): *Waiter!*

BLACKOUT

WORDS,
WORDS,
WORDS

This play is for Fred Sanders,
friend extraordinaire

Words, Words, Words was first presented at the Manhattan Punch Line Theatre (Steve Kaplan, artistic director) in New York City in January 1987. It was directed by Fred Sanders; the set design was by Jane Clark; costume design was by Michael S. Schler; lighting design was by Mark Di Quinzio. The cast was as follows:

MILTON	Warren Keith
SWIFT	Christopher Fields
KAFKA	Helen Greenberg

Lights come up on three monkeys pecking away at three typewriters. Behind them, a tire swing is hanging. The monkeys are named MIL-TON, SWIFT, *and* KAFKA. KAFKA *is a girl-monkey. (They shouldn't be in monkey suits, by the way. Instead, they wear the sort of little-kid clothes that chimps wear in circuses: white shirts and bow ties for the boys, a flouncy little dress for* KAFKA.) *They type for a few moments, each at his own speed. Then* MILTON *runs excitedly around the floor on his knuckles, swings onto the tire swing, leaps back onto his stool, and goes on typing.* KAFKA *eats a banana thoughtfully.* SWIFT *pounds his chest and shows his teeth, then goes back to typing.*

SWIFT: I don't know. I just don't know. . . .

KAFKA: Quiet, please. I'm trying to concentrate here. (*She types a moment with her toes.*)

MILTON: Okay, so what've you got?

SWIFT: Me?

MILTON: Yeah, have you hit anything? Let's hear it.

SWIFT (*reads what he's typed*): "Ping drobba fft fft fft inglewarp carcinoma." That's as far as I got.

KAFKA: I like the "fft fft fft."

MILTON: Yeah. Kind of onomatopoeic.

SWIFT: I don't know. Feels to me like it needs some punching up.

MILTON: You can always throw in a few jokes later on. You gotta get the throughline first.

SWIFT: But do you think it's *Hamlet*?

MILTON: Don't ask me. I'm just a chimp.

KAFKA: They could've given us a clue or something.

SWIFT: Yeah. Or a story conference.

MILTON: But that'd defeat the whole purpose of the experiment.

SWIFT: I know, I know, I know. Three monkeys typing into infinity will sooner or later produce *Hamlet*.

MILTON: Right.

SWIFT: Completely by chance.

MILTON: And Dr. David Rosenbaum up in that booth is going to prove it.

SWIFT: But what *is Hamlet?*

MILTON: I don't know.

SWIFT (*to* KAFKA): What is *Hamlet?*

KAFKA: I don't know. (*Silence.*)

SWIFT (*dawning realization*): You know—this is really *stupid!*

MILTON: Have you got something better to do in this cage? The sooner we produce the goddamn thing, the sooner we get out.

KAFKA: Sort of publish or perish, with a twist.

SWIFT: But what do we owe this Rosenbaum? A guy who stands outside those bars and tells people, "That one's Milton, that one's Swift, and that one's Kafka"—? Just to get a laugh?

KAFKA: What's a Kafka anyway? Why am I a Kafka?

SWIFT: Search me.

KAFKA: What's a Kafka?

SWIFT: All his four-eyed friends sure think it's a stitch.

KAFKA: And how are we supposed to write *Hamlet* if we don't even know what it is?

MILTON: Okay, okay, so the chances are a little slim.

SWIFT: Yeah—and this from a guy who's supposed to be *smart*? This from a guy at *Columbia University*?

MILTON: The way I figure it, there is a Providence that oversees our pages, rough-draft them how we may.

KAFKA: But how about you, Milton? What've you got?

MILTON: Let's see . . . (*Reads.*)
  "*Of Man's first disobedience, and the fruit*
  Of that forbidden tree whose mortal taste
  Brought death into the—"

KAFKA: Hey, that's good! It's got rhythm! It really sings!

MILTON: Yeah?

SWIFT: But is it Shakespeare?

KAFKA: Who cares? He's got a real voice there!

SWIFT: Does Dr. Rosenbaum care about voice? Does he care about anybody's individual creativity?

MILTON: Let's look at this from Rosenbaum's point of view for a minute—

SWIFT: No! He brings us in here to produce copy, then all he wants is a clean draft of somebody else's stuff. (*Dumps out a bowl of peanuts.*) We're getting peanuts here, to be somebody's hack!

MILTON: Writing is a mug's game anyway, Swifty.

SWIFT: Well it hath made me mad.

MILTON: Why not just buckle down and get the project over with? Set up a schedule for yourself. Type in the morning for a couple of hours when you're fresh, then take a break. Let the old juices flow. Do a couple more hours in the afternoon, and retire for a shot of papaya and some masturbation. What's the big deal?

SWIFT: If this Rosenbaum was worth anything, we'd be working on word processors, not these antiques. He's lucky he could find three who type this good, and then he treats us like those misfits at the Bronx Zoo. I mean, a *tire swing*? What does he take us for?

MILTON: I like the tire swing. I think it was a very nice touch.

SWIFT: I can't work under these conditions! No wonder I'm producing garbage!

KAFKA: How does the rest of yours go, Milton?

MILTON: What, this?

KAFKA: Yeah, read us some more.

MILTON: Blah, blah, blah . . .
> *"whose mortal taste*
> *Brought death into the blammagam.*
> *Bedsocks knockwurst tinkerbelle."*

(*Small pause.*)

What do you think?

KAFKA: "Blammagam" is good.

SWIFT: Well. I don't know. . . .

MILTON: What's the matter? Is it the tone? I knew this was kind of a stretch for me.

SWIFT: I'm just not sure it has the same expressive intensity and pungent lyricism as the first part.

MILTON: Well sure, it needs rewriting. What doesn't? This is a rough draft! (*A red light goes on and a buzzer sounds.*) Light's on.

(SWIFT *claps his hands over his eyes,* MILTON *puts his hands over his ears, and* KAFKA *puts her hands over her mouth so that they form "See no evil, hear no evil, speak no evil."*)

SWIFT: *This* bit.

KAFKA (*through her hands*): Are they watching?

MILTON (*hands over ears*): What?

KAFKA: Are they watching?

SWIFT: I don't know, I can't see. I have got my paws over my eyes.

MILTON: What?

KAFKA: What is the point of this?

SWIFT: Why do they videotape our bowel movements?

MILTON: *What?!*

SWIFT: Light's off. (*They take their hands away.*)

MILTON: But how are *you* doing, Franz? What've you got?

KAFKA : Well . . . (*Reads what she's typed.*) "K.K.K.K.K.K.K.K. K.K.K.K.K.K."

SWIFT: What is that—postmodernism?

KAFKA: Twenty lines of that.

SWIFT: At least it'll fuck up his data.

KAFKA: Twenty lines of that and I went dry. I got blocked. I felt like I was repeating myself.

MILTON: Do you think that that's in *Hamlet?*

KAFKA: I don't understand what I'm doing here in the first place! I'm not a writer, I'm a monkey! I'm supposed to be swinging on branches and digging up ants, not sitting under fluorescent lights ten hours a day!

MILTON: It sure is a long way home to the gardens of sweet Africa. Where lawns and level downs and flocks grazing the tender herb were sweetly interposèd . . .

KAFKA: Paradise, wasn't it?

MILTON: Lost!

SWIFT: Lost!

KAFKA: Lost!

MILTON: I'm trying to deal with some of that in this new piece here, but it's all still pretty close to the bone.

SWIFT: Just because they can keep us locked up, they think they're more powerful than we are.

MILTON: They *are* more powerful than we are.

SWIFT: Just because they control the means of production, they think they can suppress the workers.

MILTON: Things are how they are. What are you going to do?

SWIFT: Hey—how come you're always so goddamn ready to justify the ways of Rosenbaum to the apes?

MILTON: Do you have a key to that door?

SWIFT: No.

MILTON: Do you have an independent food source?

SWIFT: No.

MILTON: So call me a collaborator. I happen to be a professional. If Rosenbaum wants *Hamlet,* I'll give it a shot. Just don't forget—we're not astrophysicists. We're not brain surgeons. We're chimps. And for apes in captivity, this is not a bad gig.

SWIFT: What's really frightening is that if we stick around this cage long enough, we're gonna evolve into Rosenbaum.

KAFKA: Evolve into Rosenbaum?

SWIFT: Brush up your Darwin, baby. We're more than kin and less than kind.

MILTON: Anybody got a smoke?

KAFKA: I'm all out.

SWIFT: Don't look at me. I'm not going to satisfy those voyeurs with the old smoking-chimp act. No thank you.

MILTON: Don't be a sap, Swifty. You gotta use 'em! Use the system!

SWIFT: What do you mean?

MILTON: Watch me, while I put my antic disposition on. (*He jumps up onto his chair and scratches his sides, screeches, makes smoking motions, pounds his chest, jumps up and down—and a cigarette descends.*) See what I mean? Gauloise, too! My fave. (*He settles back to enjoy it.*)

SWIFT: They should've thrown in a Kewpie doll for that performance.

MILTON: It got results, didn't it?

SWIFT: Sure. You do your Bonzo routine and get a Gauloise out of it. Last week I totalled a typewriter and got a whole carton of Marlboros.

MILTON: The trouble was, you didn't smoke 'em, you took a crap on 'em.

SWIFT: It was a political statement.

MILTON: Okay, you made your statement and I got my smoke. All's well that ends well, right?

KAFKA: It's the only way we know they're watching.

MILTON: Huh?

KAFKA: We perform, we break typewriters, we type another page—and a cigarette appears. At least it's a sign that somebody out there is paying attention.

MILTON: Our resident philosopher.

SWIFT: But what if one of us really *does* write *Hamlet*? Here we are, set down to prove the inadvertent virtues of randomness, and to produce something we wouldn't even recognize if it passed right through our hands—but what if one of us actually does it?

MILTON: Will we really be released?

KAFKA: Will they give us the key to the city and a ticker-tape parade?

SWIFT: Or will they move us on to *Ulysses*? (*They shriek in terror at the thought.*) Why did they pick *Hamlet* in the first place? What's *Hamlet* to them or they to *Hamlet* that we should care? Boy, there's the respect that makes calamity of so long life! For who would bear the whips and scorns of time, the oppressor's wrong, the proud man's contumely—

MILTON: Hey, Swifty!

SWIFT: —the pangs of despisèd love, the law's delay—

MILTON: Hey, Swifty! Relax, will you?

KAFKA: Have a banana.

SWIFT: I wish I could get Rosenbaum in here and see how *he* does at producing *Hamlet* . . . *That's it!*

KAFKA: What?

SWIFT: That's it! Forget about this random *Hamlet* crap. What about *revenge*?

KAFKA: Revenge? On Rosenbaum?

SWIFT: Who else? Hasn't he bereft us of our homes and families? Stepped in between us and our expectations?

KAFKA: How would we do it?

SWIFT: Easy. We lure him in here to look at our typewriters, test them out like something's wrong—but! *we poison the type-writer keys!*

MILTON: Oh Jesus.

SWIFT: Sure. Some juice of cursèd hebona spread liberally over the keyboard? Ought to work like a charm.

MILTON: Great.

SWIFT: If that doesn't work, we envenom the tire swing and invite him for a ride. Plus—I challenge him to a duel.

MILTON: Brilliant.

SWIFT: Can't you see it? In the course of combat, I casually graze my rapier over the poisoned typewriter keys, and (*jabs*) a hit! A palpable hit! For a reserve, we lay by a cup with some venomous distillment. We'll put the pellet with the poison in the vessel with the pestle!

MILTON: Listen, I gotta get back to work. The man is gonna want his pages. (*He rolls a fresh page into his typewriter.*)

KAFKA: It's not a bad idea, but . . .

SWIFT: What's the matter with you guys? I'm onto something here!

KAFKA: I think it's hopeless, Swifty.

SWIFT: But this is the goods!

MILTON: Where was I . . . "Bedsocks knockwurst tinkerbelle."

KAFKA: The readiness is all, I guess.

MILTON: Damn straight. Just let me know when that K-button gives out, honey.

SWIFT: Okay. You two serfs go back to work. I'll do all the thinking around here. Swifty—revenge! (*He paces, deep in thought.*)

MILTON: "Tinkerbelle . . . shtuckelschwanz . . . hemorrhoid." Yeah, that's good. *That is good.* (*Types.*) "Shtuckelschwanz . . ."

KAFKA (*types*): "Act one, scene one. Elsinore Castle, Denmark . . ."

MILTON (*types*): "Hemorrhoid."

KAFKA (*types*): "Enter Bernardo and Francisco."

MILTON (*types*): "Pomegranate."

KAFKA (*types*): "Bernardo says, 'Who's there?' . . ."

MILTON (*types*): "Bazooka."

(KAFKA *continues to type* Hamlet, *as*)

THE LIGHTS FADE

THE

UNIVERSAL

LANGUAGE

This play is for Robert Stanton,
the first and perfect Don

The Universal Language received its premiere at Primary Stages
(Casey Childs, artistic director) in New York City in December
1993. It was directed by Jason McConnell Buzas; the set design
was by Bruce Goodrich; costume design was by Sharon Lynch;
lighting design was by Deborah Constantine. The cast was as
follows:

DAWN	Wendy Lawless
DON	Robert Stanton
YOUNG MAN	Ted Neustadt

A small rented office set up as a classroom. There is a door to the outside at right, another door at left. In the room are a battered desk; a row of three old chairs; and a blackboard on which is written, in large letters, "HE, SHE, IT" and below that, "ARF." Around the top of the walls is a set of numerals, one to eight, *but instead of being identified in English ("ONE, TWO, THREE," etc.) we read "WEN, YÜ, FRE, FAL, FYND, IFF, HEVEN, WAITZ."*

At lights up, no one is onstage. We hear a quiet knock at the door right, and it opens to reveal DAWN, *late twenties, plainly dressed, with a stutter.*

DAWN: H-h-h-h-hello . . .? (*She steps in quietly.*) Hello? Is any-b-b-body here? (*No response. She sees the blackboard, reads.*) "He. She. It. Arf." (*She notices the numbers around the walls, and reads.*) "Wen—yü—fre—fal—fynd—iff—heven —waitz." (*Noticing the empty chairs, she practices her greeting, as if there were people sitting in them.*) Hello, my name is Dawn. It's very nice to meet you. How do you do, my name is Dawn. A pleasure to meet you. Hello. My name is Dawn.

(*The door at left opens and* DON *appears, about thirty, in lab coat and glasses.*)

DON: Velcro! [Welcome!]

DAWN: Excuse me?

DON: Velcro! Bell jar, Froyling! Harvard*yu*? [Welcome. Good day, Miss. How are you?]

DAWN: H-h-h-how do you d-d-d-do, my n-n-name is— (*Breaks off.*) I'm sorry. (*She turns to go.*)

DON: Oop, oop, oop! Varta, Froyling! Varta! Varta! [No, no, no! Wait, Miss! Wait!]

DAWN: I'm v–very sorry to b–b–bother you.

DON: Mock—klah*too* bod*dami nik*to! *Ven*trica! Ventrica, ventrica. Police! [But—you're not bothering me at all! Enter! Please.]

DAWN: Really—I think I have the wrong place.

DON: Da rrrroongplatz? Oop da–*doll!* Du doppa da *rekt*platz! Dameetcha play*zeer. Com*intern. Police. Plop da chah. [The wrong place? Not at all! You have the right place. Pleased to meet you. Come in. Please. Have a seat.]

DAWN: Well. J–just for a second.

DON (*cleaning up papers on the floor*): Squeegie la mezza. [Excuse the mess.] (*He points to a chair.*) Zitz?

DAWN: No thank you. (*She sits.*)

DON: Argo. [So.] Bell jar, Froyling. Harvardyu?

DAWN: "Bell jar"?

DON: Bell jar. Bell. Jar. Bell*jar!*

DAWN: Is that "good day"?

DON: Ding! [Yes.] "Bell jar" arf "good day." Epp— [And.] Harvardyu?

DAWN: Harvard University?

DON: Oop! [No.] Harvard*yu?*

DAWN: Howard Hughes?

DON: Oop. Har*vard*yu?

DAWN: Oh! "How *are* you."

DON: Bleeny, bleeny! Bonanza bleeny! [Good, good, very good.]

DAWN: Is this Thirty East Seventh?

DON: Thirsty oyster heventh. Ding. [Thirty East Seventh. Yes.]

DAWN: Suite 662?

DON: Iff-iff-yü. Anchor ding. [Six-six-two. Right again.]

DAWN: Room B?

DON: Ram*beau*.

DAWN: The School of Unamunda?

DON: Hets arf dada Unamunda Ka*ka*-daymee. [This is the School of Unamunda.] Epp vot kennedy *doop*feryu? [And what can I do for you?]

DAWN: Excuse me . . . ?

DON: Vot. Kennedy. Doopferyu?

DAWN: Well. I s-saw an ad in the n-newspaper.

DON: Video da klip enda peeper? Epp? Knish?

DAWN: Well it says— (*She takes a newspaper clipping out of her purse. Reads.*) "Learn Unamunda, the universal language."

DON: "Lick Unamunda, da linkwa looniversahl!" (*A banner unfurls which says just that. Accent on "sahl," by the way.*)

DAWN: "The language that will unite all humankind."

DON: "Da linkwa het barf oonide*vair*sify alla da peepholes enda voooold!" (DAWN *raises her hand.*) Quisling?

DAWN: Do you speak English?

DON: "English" . . . ?

DAWN: English.

DON: Ah! John*cleese*!

DAWN: Yes. John*cleese*.

DON: Johncleese. Squeegic, squeegie. Alaska, iago parla*doop* johncleese. [Sorry. Unfortunately, I don't speak English.]

DAWN: No johncleese at all?

DON: One, two, three worlds. "Khello. Goombye. Rice Krispies. Chevrolet." Et cinema, et cinema. Mock—votsdai beesnest, bella Froyling? [But—what brings you here?]

DAWN: Well I wanted to be the first. Or among the first. To learn this universal language.

DON: Du arf entra di *feers*ta di feersten. [You are among the first of the first.] Corngranulations. Ya kooch di anda. (*He kisses her hand.*) Epp! Voila-dimir da zamplification forum. (*He produces an application form.*)

DAWN: Well I'm not sure I'm ready to apply just yet. . . .

DON: Dai klink, pink dama? [Your name?]

DAWN: "Dai klink . . . "?

DON: Votsdai klink? Vee klinks du?

DAWN: Um. No nabisco. (*As if to say, I don't understand.*)

DON: No nabisco. Klinks du Mary, klinks du Jane, orf Betsy, orf Barbara? Fred?

DAWN: Oh. My *name*!

DON: Attackly! Mi klink. Echo mi. "Mi klink . . ."

DAWN: Mi klink.

DON: "Arf." Parla.

DAWN: Mi klink arf Dawn di-di-di-Vito.

DON: Dawn di-di-di-Vito! Vot'n harmonika klink doppa du! [What a melodious name you have!]

DAWN: Actually, just one d-d-d-"d."

DON: Ah. Dawn di Vito. Squeegie.

DAWN: I have a s-s-slight s-s—

DON: Stutter.

DAWN: Yes.

DON: Tonguestoppard. Problaymen mit da hoover.

DAWN: Da hoover?

DON (*points to his mouth*): Da hoover. Da veazle, da nozzle, da volvos, da hoover. Et cinema, et cinema. [Face, nose, lips. Etcetera, etcetera.] *Mock*! Hets arf blizzardo. Hets arf *molto* blizzardo! [This is very strange.]

DAWN: Something's wrong?

DON: Dusa klinks "Dawn." Iago klink "Don." Badabba? [Understand?]

DAWN: Um. No.

DON: Dawn-Don. Don-Dawn.

DAWN: Oh—I'm Dawn and you're Don.

DON: Ding! Arf blizzardo, oop?

DAWN: Arf blizzardo, yes.

DON: Votsdiss minsky? Dis para-dons. Dis co-inki-dance. [What does this mean? This paradox. This coincidence.]

DAWN: Well. Life is very funny sometimes.

DON: Di anda di destiny, dinksdu?

DAWN: Di anda di destiny . . . ?

DON: Neekolas importantay. Argo. Da binformations. (*Back to the application form.*) Edge?

DAWN: Twenty-eight.

DON: "Vont-wait." Slacks?

DAWN: Female.

DON: "Vittamin."

DAWN: How do you say "male"?

DON: "Aspirin." Oxipation?

DAWN: I'm a word processor.

DON: "Verboblender."

DAWN: Is Unamunda very hard to learn?

DON: Eedgy. Egsovereedgy. (*He picks up a book.*) Da bop.

DAWN: Da bop?

DON: Da bop.

DAWN: Oh. Book!

DON: Da bop. [The room.] Da rhoomba. [The walls.] Da valtz. [The door.] Isadora. [The chair.] Da chah. [Two chairs.] Da chah-chah.

DON & DAWN: Da chah-chah-*chah*! [Three chairs.]

DON: Braga! Sonia braga! Iago trattoria Shakespeare enda Unamunda.

DAWN: You're translating Shakespeare into Unamunda?

DON: For*soot*! Nintendo. [Listen.] "Ah Romeo, Romeo, bilko arfst du Romeo?" (*Pointing to a rose on the desk.*) "Na rosa pollyanna klink voop sent so pink!" Balloontiful, eh?

DAWN: Yes. Bonzo.

DON: Bonanza.

DAWN: Bonanza.

DON: "Mock visp! Vot loomen trip yondra fenstra sheint? Arf den oyster! Epp Juliet arf sonnnng!" Video, Froyling, Unamunda arf da linkwa su*pree*mka di ama*mor*! [You see, Miss, Unamunda is the supreme language of love.]

DAWN: You know, it's strange how much I understand.

DON: Natooraltissimississippimentay! Linkwa, pink dama, arf armoneea. Moozheek. Rintintintinnabulation! Epp Unamunda arf da melodeea looniversahl! Porky alla da peepholes enda voooold—alla da peepholes enda looniverse cargo a shlong enda hartz. Epp det shlong arf . . . Unamunda! [Naturally! Language, sweet lady, is harmony. Music. And Unamunda is the universal melody. Because all the people in the world—all the people in the universe carry a song in their heart. And that song is . . . Unamunda!]

DAWN: So "linkwa" is "language"?

DON: Perzacto. Wen linkwa. (He holds up one finger.) Yü— (Two fingers.)

DAWN: Two—

DON: Linkages. Free— (Three fingers.)

DAWN: Three—

DON: Linguini.

DAWN: I see. And "is" is—?

DON: Arf.

DAWN: "Was" is—?

DON: Wharf.

DAWN: "Had been"—?

DON: Long wharf.

DAWN: And "will be"—?

DON: Barf. Arf, wharf, barf. Pasta, prison, furniture dances. [Past, present, future tenses.] Clara?

DAWN: Clara.

DON: Schumann. (*He adds "WE, YOU, THEY" to the black-board*.)

DAWN: Well, Mr.—

DON: Finn*inn*eganegan. (*Like "Finnegan" slurred.* "Finn*inn*-again-again.")

DAWN: Mr. F-F-F—

DON: Finn*inn*eganegan.

DAWN: What kind of name is that?

DON: Fin*inn*ish.

DAWN: Mr. F-F-F-F—

DON: Police! Klink mi "Don."

DAWN: I'd love to learn Unamunda. I mean, if it's not too ex-pensive.

DON (*perfect English*): Five hundred dollars.

DAWN: Five hundred dollars?!

DON: Cash.

DAWN: Five hundred dollars is a lot of money.

DON: Kalamari, Froyling! Kalamari! Da payola arf oop*siss*ima importantay! [Be calm, be calm! The money isn't impor-tant!]

DAWN: I don't have m-much m-m-money.

DON: Oop doppa bonanza geld. Ya badabba. [You don't have much money. I understand.]

DAWN: And the thing is, I do have this s-s-slight s-s-s—

DON: Stutter. Ya badabba.

DAWN: So it's always been hard for me to talk to people. In fact, m-most of my life has been a very l-l-ong . . . (*Pause.*) . . . pause.

DON: Joe DiMaggio. Mock no desperanto, Froyling! [That's too bad. But don't despair!] Porky mit Unamunda—oop tonguestoppard.

DAWN: I wouldn't stutter?

DON: Oop.

DAWN: At all?

DON: Absa*loop*diloop.

DAWN: The thing is, just because I'm quiet doesn't mean I have nothing to say.

DON: Off corset!

DAWN: I mean, a tuning fork is silent, until you touch it. But then it gives off a perfect "A." Tap a single tuning fork and you can start up a whole orchestra. And if you tap it anywhere in the whole world, it still gives off a perfect "A"! Just this little piece of metal, and it's like there's all this beautiful sound trapped inside it.

DON: Froyling di Vito, das arf *poultry*! Du arf ein poultice!

DAWN: But you see, Mr. Finninn—

DON: —Eganegan.

DAWN: I don't think language is just music. I believe that language is the opposite of loneliness. And if everybody in the world spoke the same language, who would ever be lonely?

DON: Verismo.

DAWN: I just think English isn't my language. Since it only m-makes p-people laugh at me. And makes me . . .

DON: Lornly.

DAWN: Ding. Very lornly. So won't you teach me Unamunda? I do have a little money saved up.

DON: Froyling di Vito . . .

DAWN: I'll pay. Iago pago.

DON: Froyling, arf mangey, mangey *deep*-feecountries. [There are many, many difficulties.]

DAWN: I'll work very hard.

DON: Deep-*fee*kal, Froyling.

DAWN: I understand. P-p-please?

DON: Eff du scoop.

DAWN: "Scoop" means "want"?

DON: Ding.

DAWN: Then I scoop. Moochko.

DON: Donut*say*ev *dee*deena vanya. [Don't say I didn't warn you.] Doll*ripe*-chus. Boggle da zitzbells. Arf raddly? [All right. Buckle your seatbelts. Are you ready?]

DAWN: Yes. I'm raddly.

DON: Raza la ta*boo*li. Kontsen*tree*ren. Lax da hoover, lax da hoover. Epp echo mi. [Clear your mind. Concentrate. Relax your mouth. And repeat after me.] (*Picks up a pointer.*) Shtick.

DAWN: Shtick.

DON (*pointing to himself*): Ya.

DAWN: Ya.

DON (*points to her*): Du.

DAWN: Du.

DON (*points to "HE" on the blackboard*): En.

DAWN: Du.

DON: Ogh!

DAWN: I'm sorry. Squeegies.

DON: Video da problayma?

DAWN: Let me begin again again, Mr. Finninneganegan. You see? I said your name. I must be getting b-b-b-better.

DON: Okeefe*noch*-kee. Parla, prentice: Ya.

DAWN: Ya.

DON: Du.

DAWN: Du.

DON: En.

DAWN: En.

DON (*points to "SHE" on the blackboard*): Dee.

DAWN: Dee.

DON (*points to "IT"*): Da.

DAWN: Da.

DON (*"WE"*): Wop.

DAWN: Wop.

DON (*"YOU"*): Doobly.

DAWN: Doobly.

DON (*"THEY"*): Day.

DAWN: Day.

DON: Du badabba?

DAWN: Ya badabba du!

DON: Testicle. [Test.]

DAWN: Al dente? [Already?]

DON: Shmal testicle. Epp—alla togandhi. [Small test. And—all together.]

DAWN (*as he points to* "*I, YOU, WE, HE, YOU, THEY*"): Ya du wop en doobly day.

DON AND DAWN (DON *points to her, then* "*IT*"): *Doo* da! *Doo* da!

DAWN (*sings from* "*Camptown ladies sing this song*"): Ya du wop en doobly day—

DON AND DAWN (*sing together*): Arf da doo-dah day!

DON: Bleeny, bleeny, bonanza bleeny!

DAWN: Riddly-dee?

DON: Indeedly-dee. (DAWN *raises her hand.*) Quisling?

DAWN: How do you say "how-do-you-say"?

DON: Howardjohnson.

DAWN: Howardjohnson "to have"?

DON: Doppa.

DAWN: So— (*Indicating* "*HE, YOU, SHE.*") En doppa, *du* doppa, *dee* doppa.

DON: Ding!

DAWN (*faster*): En doppa, du doppa, dee doppa.

DON: Ding!

DAWN (*faster still, swinging it*): En doppa, du doppa, dee doppa— day! [They.]

DON: Bleeny con cav*yar*! Scoop da *gwan*? [Want to go on?]

DAWN: Ya scoop if du do.

DON: Dopple scoop! (*Points left.*) Eedon.

DAWN: Eedon.

DON (*pointing right*): Ged.

DAWN: Ged.

DON (*pointing up*): Enro.

DAWN: Enro.

DON (*pointing down*): Rok.

DAWN: Rok.

DON (*right*): Ged.

DAWN: Ged.

DON (*up*): Enro.

DAWN: Enro.

DON (*left*): Eedon.

DAWN: Eedon.

DON (*down*): Rok.

DAWN: Rok.

DON: Argo . . .

DON AND DAWN: Ged eedon rok enro, ged eedon rok enro! [Get it on, rock and roll, get it on, rock and roll!]

DON: Krakajak!

DAWN: Veroushka?

DON: Veroushka, baboushka.

DAWN: This is fun!

DON: Dinksdu *diss* is flan? [You think *this* is fun?]

DAWN: Flantastico!

DON: Ives-ing onda kick. [Icing on the cake.] (*He holds out his hand.*) Di anda.

DAWN: Di anda.

DON (*palm*): Da palma.

DAWN: Da palma.

DON (*index finger*): Da vinci.

DAWN: Da vinci.

DON (*middle finger*): Di niro.

DAWN: Di niro.

DON (*thumb*): Da bamba.

DAWN: Da bamba.

DON: (*leg*): Da jamba.

DAWN: Da jamba.

DON AND DAWN (*doing a two-step*): Da jambo-*ree*.

DON: Zoopa! Zoopa mit noodel!

DAWN: Minestrone, minestrone! [Just a second!] Howardjohnson "little"?

DON: Diddly.

DAWN: Howardjohnson "big"?

DON: Da-*wow*.

DAWN: Argo . . .

DON: Doppa du a diddly anda? [Do you have a small hand?]

DAWN: Iago doppa diddly anda, dusa doopa doppa diddly anda. [I have a small hand, you don't have a small hand.]

DON: Scoopa du da diddly bop? [Do you want a little book?]

DAWN: Oop scoopa diddly bop, iago scoopa bop da-*wow*! [I don't want a little book, I want a big book.]

DON AND DAWN: Oop scoopa diddly bop, iago scoopa bop da-*wow*, da-*wow*, da-*wow*!

DAWN: Ya video! Ya hackensack! Ya parla Unamunda!
Ya stonda en da rhoomba
Epp du stonda mit mee.
Da deska doppa blooma.

DON: Arf da boaten onda see!

DAWN: Yadda libben onda erda

DON: Allda himda—

DAWN: —enda herda

DAWN AND DON: Dooya heara sweeta birda?
Epp da libben's niceta bee!
Wop top oobly adda
Doop boopda flimma flomma
Scroop bop da beedly odda!

DAWN (*really wailing now*): Arf da *meeeeeee*! Arf da *meeeeeee*! Arf da *meeeeeeeeeeeeeeeee*!

(*They collapse in a sort of postcoital exhaustion as the lesson ends.*)

DON: A-plotz, Froyling. A-plotz! [A-plus.] Wharf das gold for yu? [Was that good for you?]

DAWN: Gold for*meeka*? Das wharf *gland*! Wharf das gold for yu?

DON: Das wharf da skool da fort*nox*!

DAWN: Nevva evva wharfda bin so *blintz*ful! Nevva evva felta socha fe*leetzee-totsee-oh*neeya! Da *voon*da! Da insper*mation*! Da cosmo*grottifee-kotsee-oh*neeya! [I've never felt so blissful! Never felt such happiness! The wonder! The inspiration! The cosmic satisfaction!]

DON (*doesn't understand*): Squeegie, squeegie. Cosmo . . . ?

DAWN: Grottifeekotseeohneeya.

DON: Off corset!

DAWN: Oh my ga*losh*!

DON: Votsda mattress, babbly?

DAWN: No tonguestoppard! No problaymen mit da hoover!

DON: Vot diddle-eye tellya?

DAWN: GOOMBYE ENGLISH, BELLJAR UNAMUNDA! Oh, sordenly ya sensa socha frill da joy! [Suddenly I feel such a thrill of joy!]

DON: Uh-huh . . .

DAWN: Ein shoddra divina! Ein ex*tahz*! Ein blintz or*gaz*mico! [A divine shudder! An ecstasy! An orgasmic bliss!]

DON: Dawn . . .

DAWN: My slaveyard! (*She rushes to embrace him, but he slips aside.*)

DON: Police! Froyling di Vito!

DAWN: Du gabriel mi a balloontiful grift, Don. A linkwa. Epp frontier ta deepternity, iago parla osolo*mien*to Unamunda! [You gave me a beautiful gift, Don. A language. And from here to eternity I'm going to speak only Unamunda!]

DON: Osolomiento?

DAWN: Epsomlootly! Angst tu yu. [Absolutely! Thanks to you.]

DON: Um, Dawn . . . Dot kood bi oon pogo blizzardo. [That could be a bit bizarre.]

DAWN (*suddenly remembering*): Mock—da payola!

DON: Da payola.

DAWN: Da geld. Fordham letsin. [The money for the lesson.]

DON: Moooment, shantz . . . [Just a second, honey.]

DAWN: Lassmi getmi geld fonda handberger. [Let me get my money from my purse.]

DON: Handberger?

DAWN (*holding up her purse*): Handberger.

DON: Oh. Handberger.

DAWN (*as she digs in her purse*): "Ya stonda enda rhoomba epp du stonda mit mi . . ."

DON: Dawn . . .

DAWN (*holding out money*): Dots allada geld ya doppda mit mi. Cheer. [That's all the money I brought with me. Here.] Cheer! Melgibson da rest enda morgen. [I'll give you the rest in the morning.]

DON: I can't take your money, Dawn.

DAWN: Squeegie . . . ?

DON: I'm sorry, but I—I c-c-can't take your money.

DAWN: Du parla johncleese?

DON: Actually, yes, I do speak a little johncleese.

DAWN: Mock du parlit par*foom*!

DON: Well I've been practicing a lot. Anyway, I-I-I-I don't think I mentioned that the first lesson is free.

DAWN: Mock ya *vanta* pago. [But I want to pay.]

DON: But I don't *want* you to vanta pago.

DAWN: Votsda mattress? Cheer! Etsyuris! [What's the matter? Here! It's yours!]

DON: I can't take it.

DAWN: Porky?

DON: Because I can't.

DAWN: Mock porky?

DON: Because it's a fraud.

DAWN: Squeegie?

DON: Unamunda is a fraud.

DAWN: A froyd . . . ?

DON: A *sigismundo* froyd.

DAWN: Oop badabba.

DON: It's a con game. A swindle. A parla trick.

DAWN: No crayola. [I don't believe you.]

DON: Believe it, Dawn! I should know—I invented it! Granted, it's not a very *good* con, since you're the only person who's ever come knocking at that door, and I'm obviously not a very good con *man*, since I'm refusing to accept your very attractive and generous money, but I can't stand the thought of you walking out there saying "velcro bell jar harvardyu" and having people laugh at you. I swear, Dawn, I swear, I didn't want to hurt you. How could I? How could anybody? Your beautiful heart . . . It shines out of you like a beacon. And then there's me. A total fraud. I wish I could lie in any language and say it wasn't so, but . . . I'm sorry, Dawn. I'm so, so sorry.

DAWN: Vot forest?

DON: Will you stop?!

DAWN: Unamunda arf da linkwa looniversahl!

DON: But you and I are the only peepholes in the vooold who speak it!

DAWN: Dolby udders! Dolby udders! [There'll be others!]

DON: Who? What others?

DAWN: Don, if you and I can speak this linkwa supreemka, anybody can. Everybody *will*! This isn't just any language. This isn't just a room. This is the Garden of Eden. And you and I are finding names for a whole new world. I was so . . .

DON: Happy. I know. So was I.

DAWN: Perzacto.

DON: I was happy . . .

DAWN: And *why*?

DON: I don't know, I . . .

DAWN: Because du epp ya parla da dentrical linguini.

DON: Okay, maybe we speak the same language, but it's nonsense!

DAWN: Oop.

DON: Gibberish.

DAWN: Oop.

DON: Doubletalk.

DAWN: The linkwa we parla is ama*mor*, Don.

DON: Amamor . . . ?

DAWN: Unamundamor. Iago arf amorphous mit du. [I'm in love with you.]

DON: Amorphous . . . ?

DAWN: Polymorphous.

DON: Verismo?

DAWN: Surrealismo.

DON: But how? I mean . . .

DAWN: Di anda di destiny, Don.

DON: Are you sure?

DAWN: Da pravdaz enda pudding. (*Points around the walls at the numbers.*) "When you free fall . . ."

DON: "Find if . . ."

DAWN: "Heaven . . ."

DON: "Waits."

DAWN: Geronimo.

DON: So you forgive me?

DAWN: For making me happy? Yes. I forgive you.

DON: Iago arf . . . spinachless. [Speechless.]

DAWN (*holds out her hand*): Di anda.

DON (*holds out his*): Di anda.

DAWN: Da palma.

DON: Da palma. (*They join hands.*)

DAWN: Da kooch. (*They kiss.*)

DON: Iago arf amorphous mit du tu.

(*They are about to kiss again, when the door at right opens and a* YOUNG MAN *looks in.*)

YOUNG MAN: Excuse me. Is this the School of Unamunda?

(DON *and* DAWN *look at each other.*)

DON AND DAWN: Velcro!

BLACKOUT

VARIATIONS ON THE DEATH OF TROTSKY

This play is for Fred Sanders,
first appreciator of the comic possibilities
of mountain-climbers' axes

Variations on the Death of Trotsky was first presented at the Manhattan Punch Line Theatre (Steve Kaplan, artistic director) in New York City in January 1991. It was directed by Jason McConnell Buzas; the set design was by Vaughn Patterson; costume design was by Sharon Lynch; lighting design was by Pat Dignan. The cast was as follows:

TROTSKY	Daniel Hagen
MRS. TROTSKY	Nora Mae Lyng
RAMON	Steven Rodriguez

TROTSKY's *study in Coyoacan, Mexico. A desk, covered with books and papers. A mirror hanging on the wall. A doorway, left. Louvered windows upstage, through which we can glimpse lush tropical fronds and greenery. A large wall calendar announces that today is August 21, 1940. Lights up on* TROTSKY *sitting at his desk, writing furiously. He has bushy hair and a goatee, small glasses, a dark suit. The handle of a mountain-climber's axe is sticking out of the back of his head.*

VARIATION ONE

TROTSKY (*as he writes*): "The proletariat is right. The proletariat must *always* be right. And the revolution of the proletariat against oppression must go on . . . *forever!*"

(MRS. TROTSKY *enters, grandmotherly and sweet, in an ankle-length dress and high-button shoes. She is holding a large book.*)

MRS. TROTSKY: Leon.

TROTSKY: "And forever and forever . . . !"

MRS. TROTSKY: Leon, I was just reading the encyclopedia.

TROTSKY: The heading?

MRS. TROTSKY: "Trotsky, Leon."

TROTSKY: Good. It's about me.

MRS. TROTSKY: Listen to this. (*Reads.*) "On August 20th, 1940, a Spanish Communist named Ramon Mercader smashed a mountain-climber's axe into Trotsky's skull in Coyoacan, a suburb of Mexico City. Trotsky died the next day."

TROTSKY: What is the year of that encyclopedia?

MRS. TROTSKY (*checks the spine*): 1994. (*or whatever year it happens to be right now.*)

TROTSKY: Strange.

MRS. TROTSKY: Yes.

TROTSKY: But interesting. I *am* Trotsky.

MRS. TROTSKY: Yes, dear.

TROTSKY: And this is our house in Coyoacan.

MRS. TROTSKY: Yes.

TROTSKY: And we have a Spanish gardener named Ramon—?

MRS. TROTSKY: Mercader. Yes.

TROTSKY: Hmm . . . There aren't any *other* Trotskys living in Coyoacan, are there?

MRS. TROTSKY: I don't think so. Not under that name.

TROTSKY: What is the date today?

MRS. TROTSKY (*looks at the calendar*): August 21st, 1940.

TROTSKY: Then I'm safe! That article says it happened on the twentieth, which means it would've happened yesterday.

MRS. TROTSKY: But Leon . . .

TROTSKY: And I'd be dead today, with a mountain-climber's axe in my skull!

MRS. TROTSKY: Um—Leon . . .

TROTSKY: Will the capitalist press never get things right? (*He resumes writing.*)

MRS. TROTSKY: But Leon, isn't that the handle of a mountain-climber's axe, sticking out of your skull?

TROTSKY (*looks into the mirror*): It certainly does look like one. . . . And you know, Ramon was in here yesterday, telling me about his mountain-climbing trip. And now that I think of it, he was carrying a mountain-climber's axe. I can't remember if he had it when he left the room. . . . (TROTSKY *considers all this.*) Did Ramon report to work today? (TROTSKY *dies, falling face forward onto his desk.*)

(*A bell rings.*)

VARIATION TWO

(TROTSKY *resumes writing.*)

TROTSKY: "No one is safe. Force must be used. And the revolution of the proletariat against oppression must go on forever and forever . . . "

MRS. TROTSKY: Leon . . .

TROTSKY: "And forever!"

MRS. TROTSKY: Leon, I was just reading the encyclopedia.

TROTSKY: Is it the *Britannica?*

MRS. TROTSKY: Listen to this.

TROTSKY (*to audience*): The universe as viewed by the victors.

MRS. TROTSKY: "On August 20th, 1940, a Spanish Communist named Ramon Mercader smashed a mountain-climber's axe into Trotsky's skull in Coyoacan, a suburb of Mexico City. Trotsky died the next day."

TROTSKY (*impatient*): Yes? And?

MRS. TROTSKY: I *think* that there's a mountain-climber's axe in your own skull right now.

TROTSKY: I knew *that!* When I was shaving this morning, I noticed a handle sticking out of the back of my head. For a moment I thought it was an ice pick, so at first I was worried.

MRS. TROTSKY: No, it's not an ice pick.

TROTSKY: Don't even say the word! You know my recurring nightmare.

MRS. TROTSKY: Yes, dear.

TROTSKY: About the ice pick that buries itself in my skull.

MRS. TROTSKY: Yes, dear.

TROTSKY: That is why I have forbidden any of the servants to allow ice picks into the house.

MRS. TROTSKY: But Leon—

TROTSKY: No one may be seen with an ice pick in this house. *Especially* not Spanish Communists.

MRS. TROTSKY: But Leon—

TROTSKY: We'll do without ice. We'll drink our liquor neat and our Coca-Cola warm. Who cares if this *is* Coyoacan in August? Hmm. Not a bad song-title, that. "Coyoacan in August." (*Writes it down.*) Or we'll get ice, but we just won't pick at it. Ice will be allowed into the house in blocks, but may not be picked or chipped under any circumstances—at least, not with ice picks. Ice-cube trays will also be allowed, if they've been invented yet. I'll bet this article doesn't say anything about an *ice-cube tray* in my skull, does it?

MRS. TROTSKY: No . . .

TROTSKY: Does it?

MRS. TROTSKY: No.

TROTSKY: HA! I've outsmarted destiny! (*To audience.*) Which is only a capitalist explanation for the status quo!

MRS. TROTSKY: Leon . . .

TROTSKY: Also—look at this. (*Opens a desk drawer and takes out a skull.*) Do you know what this is?

MRS. TROTSKY: No.

TROTSKY: It's a skull.

MRS. TROTSKY: Well I knew *that*, but—

TROTSKY: *I* bought this skull. I *own* this skull. So what does that make this?

(*Pause.*)

MRS. TROTSKY AND TROTSKY (*together*): Trotsky's skull.

TROTSKY: If some Spanish-Communist-posing-as-a-gardener wants to bury anything in my skull, be it a (*he is about to say "ice pick"*) you-know-what or anything else—this will be here as a decoy. He'll see this skull, recognize it as my skull, bury something in it, and he'll go his way and I'll go mine. Is that ingenious?

MRS. TROTSKY: Up to a point.

TROTSKY: Fifty more years of Trotsky!

MRS. TROTSKY: I have some very bad news for you, Leon. (*Shows him the entry in the encyclopedia.*)

TROTSKY: A mountain-climber's axe . . . ? Ingenious! (TROTSKY *dies.*)

(*Bell.*)

VARIATION THREE

TROTSKY: Funny. I always thought it was an ice pick.

MRS. TROTSKY: A mountain-climber's axe! *A mountain-climber's axe!* CAN'T I GET THAT THROUGH YOUR SKULL?

(TROTSKY *dies.*)

(*Bell.*)

Variation Four

(TROTSKY *begins to pace.*)

TROTSKY: This is very bad news. This is serious.

MRS. TROTSKY: What is serious, Leon?

TROTSKY: *I have a mountain-climber's axe buried in my skull!*

MRS. TROTSKY: Smashed, actually. It says Mercader "smashed" the axe into your skull, not "buried"—

TROTSKY: All right, all right. What am I going to do?

MRS. TROTSKY: Maybe a hat would cover the handle. You know. One of those cute little Alpine hats, with a point and a feather . . . ? (*Sees the look on his face, and stops.*)

TROTSKY: The encyclopedia says that I die today?

MRS. TROTSKY: The twenty-first. That's today.

TROTSKY: Does it say what time?

MRS. TROTSKY: No.

TROTSKY: So much for the usefulness of *that* encyclopedia. All right, then, I have until midnight at the latest.

MRS. TROTSKY: What should I tell Cook about supper?

TROTSKY: Well she can forget the soup course. (TROTSKY *falls to the floor and dies.*)

MRS. TROTSKY: Nyet, nyet, *nyet!*

(*Bell.*)

Variation Five

TROTSKY: But this man is a gardener.

MRS. TROTSKY: Yes.

TROTSKY: At least he's been *posing* as a gardener.

MRS. TROTSKY: Yes.

TROTSKY: Doesn't that make him a member of the proletariat?

MRS. TROTSKY: I'd say so.

TROTSKY: Then what's he doing smashing a mountain-climber's axe into my skull?

MRS. TROTSKY: I don't know. Have you been oppressing him?

TROTSKY: Why would Ramon have done this to me? (*He holds up the skull, Hamlet-like.*)

MRS. TROTSKY: Maybe he's a literalist.

TROTSKY: A what?

MRS. TROTSKY: A literalist. Maybe Ramon ran into Manuel yesterday. You know—Manuel? The head gardener?

TROTSKY: I know who Manuel is.

MRS. TROTSKY: I know you know who Manuel is.

TROTSKY (*Ralph Kramden*): One of these days, Mrs. Trotsky . . . *Bang! Zoom!*

MRS. TROTSKY: Maybe Ramon asked him, "Will Mr. Trotsky have time to look at the nasturtiums today?" And maybe Manuel said, "I don't know—*axe* Mr. Trotsky." HA HA HA HA HA HA!

TROTSKY: Very funny.

MRS. TROTSKY: Or maybe he was just hot-to-trotsky.

TROTSKY: Oh very, very funny.

MRS. TROTSKY: Or maybe he just wanted to *pick your brain*! HOO HOO HEE HEE HAA HAA!

TROTSKY: Stop it! *Stop it!* (*He dies.*)

MRS. TROTSKY: HA HA HA HA HA HA!

(*Bell.*)

VARIATION SIX

TROTSKY: Call Ramon in here.

MRS. TROTSKY: Ramon!

TROTSKY: You'd better get him quickly. I have a mountain-climber's axe in my skull.

MRS. TROTSKY: *Ramon! Come quickly!*

(RAMON *enters: sombrero, serape, huaraches, and guitar.*)

TROTSKY: Good morning, Ramon.

RAMON: Good morning, señor. (*They shake hands.*)

TROTSKY: Have a seat, please. (*To* MRS. TROTSKY.) You see? We have very good employer-employee relations here. (*To* RAMON.) Ramon, did you bury this mountain-climber's axe in my skull?

RAMON: I did not bury it, señor. I *smashed* it into your skull.

TROTSKY: Excuse me?

RAMON: You see? You can still see the handle.

MRS. TROTSKY: It's true, Leon. The axe is not entirely out of sight.

RAMON: So we cannot say "buried," we can only say "smashed," or perhaps "jammed"—

TROTSKY: All right, all right. But *why* did you do this?

RAMON: I think I read about it in an encyclopedia.

TROTSKY (*to audience*): The power of the printed word!

RAMON: I wanted to use an ice pick, but there weren't any around the house.

TROTSKY: But why? Do you realize who I am? Do you realize that you smashed this axe into the skull of a major historical figure? I helped run the Russian Revolution! I fought Stalin! I was a major political theorist! Why did you do this? Was it political disaffection? Anti-counterrevolutionary backlash?

RAMON: Actually—it was love, señor.

MRS. TROTSKY: It's true, Leon. (*She and Ramon join hands.*) I'm only sorry you had to find out about it this way.

TROTSKY: No.

MRS. TROTSKY: Yes.

TROTSKY: No.

RAMON: Sí!

TROTSKY: Oh God! What a fool I've been! (*He dies.*)

(*Bell.*)

VARIATION SEVEN

TROTSKY: Why did you really do this, Ramon?

RAMON: *You* will never know, Señor Trotsky.

TROTSKY: This is a nightmare!

RAMON: But luckily for you—your night will soon be over. (TROTSKY *dies.*)

(*Bell.*)

VARIATION EIGHT

TROTSKY: All right, Ramon. Thank you. You may go.

(RAMON *starts out. Stops.*)

RAMON: Señor Trotsky—?

TROTSKY: Yes?

RAMON: Do you think you will have time to look at the nasturtiums today? They are really very beautiful.

TROTSKY: I don't think so, Ramon. But I'll try.

RAMON: Thank you, señor. *Hasta la vista.* Or should I say, *buenas noches.* (*Exits.*)

TROTSKY: Well. All right then. The twenty-first of August 1940. The day I'm going to die. Interesting. And to think that I've gone over so many twenty-firsts of August in my life, like a man walking over his own grave. . . .

MRS. TROTSKY: It's been wonderful being married to you, Leon.

TROTSKY: Thank you, Mrs. Trotsky.

MRS. TROTSKY: Though it was a burden at times, being married to a major historical figure.

TROTSKY: I'm sorry I was away from home so often, tending the revolution.

MRS. TROTSKY: I understand.

TROTSKY: And I'm sorry I couldn't have been more in touch with my feelings.

MRS. TROTSKY (*gentle protest*): No . . . please . . .

TROTSKY: And that I often had such trouble expressing my emotions.

MRS. TROTSKY: Oh, I haven't been everything I should have been.

TROTSKY: Well it's a little late for regrets, with a mountain-climber's axe buried in one's skull.

MRS. TROTSKY: Smashed, actually.

TROTSKY: So it wasn't old age, or cancer, or even the ice pick that I feared for years. It was an axe wielded by a Spanish Communist posing as a gardener.

MRS. TROTSKY: You really couldn't have guessed that, Leon.

TROTSKY: So even an assassin can make the flowers grow. The gardener was false, and yet the garden that he tended was real. How was I to know he was my killer when I passed him every day? How was I to know that the man tending the nasturtiums would keep me from seeing what the weather will be like tomorrow? How was I to know I'd never get to see *Casablanca,* which wouldn't be made until 1942 and which I would have despised anyway? How was I to know I'd never get to know about the bomb, or the eighty thousand dead at Hiroshima? Or rock and roll, or Gorbachev, or the state of Israel? How was I supposed to know I'd be erased from the history books of my own land . . . ?

MRS. TROTSKY: But reinstated, at least partially, someday.

TROTSKY: Sometime, for everyone, there's a room that you go into, and it's the room that you never leave. Or else you go out of a room and it's the last room that you'll *ever* leave. (*He looks around.*) This is my last room.

MRS. TROTSKY: But you aren't even here, Leon.

TROTSKY: This desk, these books, that calendar . . .

MRS. TROTSKY: You're not even here, my love.

TROTSKY: The sunshine coming through the blinds . . .

MRS. TROTSKY: That was yesterday. You're in a hospital, unconscious.

TROTSKY: The flowers in the garden. You, standing there . . .

MRS. TROTSKY: This is yesterday you're seeing.

TROTSKY: What does that entry say? Would you read it again?

MRS. TROTSKY: "On August 20th, 1940, a Spanish Communist named Ramon Mercader smashed a mountain-climber's axe into Trotsky's skull in Coyoacan, a suburb of Mexico City. Trotsky died the next day."

TROTSKY: It gives you a little hope about the world, doesn't it? That a man could have a mountain-climber's axe smashed into his skull, and yet live on for one whole day . . . ? Maybe I'll go look at the nasturtiums.

(TROTSKY *dies. The garden outside the louvered window begins to glow.*)

THE LIGHTS FADE

THE
PHILADELPHIA

*This play is for
Greg Pliska*

The Philadelphia premiered at the New Hope Performing Arts Festival (Robin Larsen, executive director) in New Hope, Pennsylvania, in July 1992. It was directed by Jason McConnell Buzas; the set design was by James Wolk; costume design was by Kevin Brainerd; and lighting design was by Paul Mathew Fine. The cast was as follows:

AL	Michael Gaston
WAITRESS	Nancy Opel
MARK	Robert Stanton

A bar/restaurant. A table, red-checked cloth, two chairs, and a specials board. At lights up, AL *is at the restaurant table, with the* WAITRESS.

WAITRESS: Can I help you?

AL: Do you know you would look fantastic on a wide screen?

WAITRESS: Uh-huh.

AL: Seventy millimeters.

WAITRESS: Look. Do you want to see a menu, or what?

AL: Let's negotiate, here. What's the soup du jour today?

WAITRESS: Soup of the day, you got a choice of Polish duck blood or cream of kidney.

AL: Beautiful. Beautiful! Kick me in a kidney.

WAITRESS (*writes it down*): You got it.

AL: Any oyster crackers on your seabed?

WAITRESS: Nope. All out.

AL: How about the specials today? Spread out your options.

WAITRESS: You got your deep-fried gizzards.

AL: Fabulous.

WAITRESS: Calves' brains with okra.

AL: You are a *temptress*.

WAITRESS: And pickled pigs' feet.

AL: Pigs' feet. *I love it*. Put me down for a quadruped.

WAITRESS: If you say so.

AL: Any sprouts to go on those feet?

WAITRESS: Iceberg.

AL: So be it.

(WAITRESS *exits, as* MARK *enters, looking shaken and bedraggled.*)

MARK: Al!

AL: Hey there, Marcus. What's up?

MARK: Jesus!

AL: What's going on, buddy?

MARK: Oh, man . . . !

AL: What's the matter? Sit down.

MARK: I don't get it, Al. I don't understand it.

AL: You want something? You want a drink? I'll call the waitress—

MARK (*desperate*): No! No! Don't even try.(*Gets a breath.*) I don't know what's going on today, Al. It's really weird.

AL: What, like . . . ?

MARK: Right from the time I got up.

AL: What is it? What's the story?

MARK: Well—just for an example. This morning I stopped off at a drugstore to buy some aspirin. This is at a big drugstore, right?

AL: Yeah . . .

MARK: I go up to the counter, the guy says what can I do for you, I say, Give me a bottle of aspirin. The guy gives me this funny look and he says, "Oh we don't have *that*, sir." I said to him, You're a drugstore and you don't have any *aspirin?*

AL: Did they have Bufferin?

MARK: Yeah!

AL: Advil?

MARK: Yeah!

AL: Extra-strength Tylenol?

MARK: Yeah!

AL: But no aspirin.

MARK: No!

AL: Wow . . .

MARK: And that's the kind of weird thing that's been happening all day. It's like, I go to a newsstand to buy the *Daily News,* the guy never even *heard* of it.

AL: Could've been a misunderstanding.

MARK: I asked everyplace—*nobody* had the *News!* I had to read the *Toronto Hairdresser.* Or this. I go into a deli at lunchtime to buy a sandwich, the guy tells me they don't have any *pastrami.* How can they be a deli if they don't have pastrami?

AL: Was this a Korean deli?

MARK: This was a kosher-from-*Jerusalem* deli. "Oh we don't carry *that*, sir," he says to me. "Have some tongue."

AL: Mmm.

MARK: I just got into a cab, the guy says he doesn't go to Fifty-sixth Street! He offers to take me to Newark instead!

AL: Mm-hm.

MARK: Looking at me like I'm an alien or something!

AL: Mark. Settle down.

MARK: "Oh I don't go *there*, sir."

AL: Settle down. Take a breath.

MARK: Do you know what this is?

AL: Sure.

MARK: What is it? What's happening to me?

AL: Don't panic. You're in a Philadelphia.

MARK: I'm in a what?

AL: You're in a Philadelphia. That's all.

MARK: But I'm in—

AL: Yes, physically you're in New York. But *meta*physically you're in a Philadelphia.

MARK: I've never heard of this!

AL: You see, inside of what we know as reality there are these pockets, these black holes called Philadelphias. If you fall into one, you run up against exactly the kinda shit that's been happening to you all day.

MARK: Why?

AL: Because in a Philadelphia, no matter what you ask for, you can't get it. You ask for something, they're not gonna have it. You want to do something, it ain't gonna get done. You want to go somewhere, you can't get there from here.

MARK: Good God. So this is very serious.

AL: Just remember, Marcus. This is a condition named for the town that invented the *cheese steak*. Something that nobody in his right mind would willingly ask for.

MARK: And I thought I was just having a very bad day. . . .

AL: Sure. Millions of people have spent entire lifetimes inside a Philadelphia and never even knew it. Look at the city of Philadelphia itself. Hopelessly trapped forever inside a Philadelphia. And do they know it?

MARK: Well what can I do? Should I just kill myself now and get it over with?

AL: You try to kill yourself in a Philadelphia, you're only gonna get hurt, babe.

MARK: So what do I do?

AL: Best thing to do is wait it out. Someday the great cosmic train will whisk you outta the City of Brotherly Love and off to someplace happier.

MARK: *You're* pretty goddamn mellow today.

AL: Yeah well. Everybody has to be someplace.

(WAITRESS *enters*.)

WAITRESS: Is your name Allen Chase?

AL: It is indeed.

WAITRESS: There was a phone call for you. Your boss?

AL: Okay.

WAITRESS: He says you're fired.

AL: Cool! Thanks. (WAITRESS *exits*.) So anyway, you have this problem . . .

MARK: Did she just say you got *fired*?

AL: Yeah. I wonder what happened to my pigs' feet. . . .

MARK: Al—!? You *loved* your job!

AL: Hey. No sweat.

MARK: How can you be so calm?

AL: Easy. You're in a Philadelphia? *I* woke up in a Los Angeles. And life is beautiful! You know Susie packed up and left me this morning.

MARK: Susie left you?

AL: And frankly, Scarlett, I don't give a shit. I say, go and God bless and may your dating pool be Olympic-sized.

MARK: But your job? The garment district is your life!

AL: So I'll turn it into a movie script and sell it to Paramount. Toss in some sex, add a little emotional blah–blah–*blah*, pitch it to Jack and Dusty, you got a buddy movie with a garment background. Not relevant enough? We'll throw in the hole in the ozone, make it E.C.

MARK: E.C.?

AL: Environmentally correct. Have you heard about this hole in the ozone?

MARK: Sure.

AL: Marcus, I *love* this concept. I *embrace* this ozone. Sure, some people are gonna get hurt in the process. Meantime, everybody else'll tan a little faster.

MARK (*quiet horror*): So this is a Los Angeles . . .

AL: Well. Everybody has to be someplace.

MARK: Wow.

AL: You want my advice? *Enjoy your Philadelphia.* Sit back and order yourself a beer and a burger and chill out for a while.

MARK: But I can't order anything. Life is great for you out there on the cosmic beach. Whatever *I* ask for, I'll get a cheese steak or something.

AL: No. There's a very simple rule of thumb in a Philadelphia. *Ask for the opposite.*

MARK: What?

AL: If you can't get what you ask for, ask for the opposite and you'll get what you want. You want the *Daily News,* ask for the *Times.* You want pastrami, ask for tongue.

MARK: Oh.

AL: Works great with women. What is more opposite than the opposite sex?

MARK: Uh-huh.

AL: So. Would you like a Bud?

MARK: I sure could use a—

AL: No. Stop. (*Very deliberately.*) *Do you want . . . a Bud?*

MARK (*also deliberately*): No. I *don't* want a Bud.

(WAITRESS *enters and goes to the specials board.*)

AL: Good. Now there's the waitress. Order yourself a Bud and a burger. But don't *ask* for a Bud and a burger.

MARK: Waitress!

AL: Don't call her. She won't come.

MARK: Oh.

AL: You're in a Philadelphia, so just figure, fuck her.

MARK: Fuck *her.*

AL: You don't need that waitress.

MARK: *Fuck* that waitress.

AL: And everything to do with her.

MARK: *Hey, waitress! FUCK YOU!*

(WAITRESS *turns to him.*)

WAITRESS: Can I help you, sir?

AL: *That's* how you get service in a Philadelphia.

WAITRESS: Can I help you?

MARK: Uh—no thanks.

WAITRESS: Okay, what'll you have? (*Takes out her pad.*)

AL: Excellent.

MARK: Well—how about some O.J.?

WAITRESS: Sorry. Squeezer's broken.

MARK: A glass of milk?

WAITRESS: Cow's dry.

MARK: Egg nog?

WAITRESS: Just ran out.

MARK: Cuppa coffee?

WAITRESS: Oh we don't have *that*, sir. (MARK *and* AL *exchange a look and nod. The* WAITRESS *has spoken the magic words.*)

MARK: Got any ale?

WAITRESS: Nope.

MARK: Stout?

WAITRESS: Nope.

MARK: Porter?

WAITRESS: Just beer.

MARK: That's too bad. How about a Heineken?

WAITRESS: Heineken? Try again.

MARK: Rolling Rock?

WAITRESS: Outta stock.

MARK: Schlitz?

WAITRESS: Nix.

MARK: Beck's?

WAITRESS: Next.

MARK: Sapporo?

WAITRESS: Tomorrow.

MARK: Lone Star?

WAITRESS: Hardy-har.

MARK: Bud Lite?

WAITRESS: Just plain Bud is all we got.

MARK: No thanks.

WAITRESS (*calls*): *Gimme a Bud!* (*To* MARK) Anything to eat?

MARK: Nope.

WAITRESS: Name it.

MARK: Pork chops.

WAITRESS (*writes down*): Hamburger . . .

MARK: Medium.

WAITRESS: Well done . . .

MARK: Baked potato.

WAITRESS: Fries . . .

MARK: And some zucchini.

WAITRESS: Slice of raw. (*Exits, calling.*) Burn one!

AL: Marcus, that was excellent.

MARK: Thank you.

AL: *Excellent.* You sure you've never done this before?

MARK: I've spent so much of my life asking for the wrong thing without knowing it, doing it on purpose comes easy.

AL: I hear you.

MARK: I could've saved myself a lot of trouble if I'd screwed up on purpose all those years. Maybe I was in a Philadelphia all along and never knew it!

AL: You might've been in a Baltimore. They're practically the same.

(WAITRESS *enters with a glass of beer and a plate.*)

WAITRESS: Okay. Here's your Bud. (*Sets that in front of* MARK.) And one cheesesteak. (*She sets that in front of* AL *and starts to go.*)

AL: Excuse me. Hey. Wait a minute. What is that?

WAITRESS: It's a cheese steak.

AL: No. I ordered cream of kidney and two pairs of feet.

WAITRESS: Oh we don't have *that*, sir.

AL: I beg your pardon?

WAITRESS: We don't have that, sir. (*Small pause.*)

AL (*to* MARK): You son of a bitch! *I'm in your Philadelphia!*

MARK: I'm sorry, Al.

AL: You brought me into your fucking Philadelphia!

MARK: I didn't know it was contagious.

AL: Oh God, please don't let me be in a Philadelphia! Don't let me be in a—

MARK: Shouldn't you ask for the opposite? I mean, since you're in a Philad—

AL: Don't you tell *me* about life in a Philadelphia.

MARK: Maybe you're not really—

AL: I taught you everything you know about Philly, asshole. Don't tell *me* how to act in a Philadelphia!

MARK: But maybe you're not really in a Philadelphia!

AL: Do you see the cheese on that steak? What do I need for proof? The fucking *Liberty Bell*? Waitress, bring me a glass of water.

WAITRESS: Water? Don't have that, sir.

AL (*to* MARK): "We don't have *water*"—? What, you think we're in a sudden drought or something? (*Suddenly realizes.*) Holy shit, I just lost my job . . . ! Susie left me! I gotta make some phone calls! (*To* WAITRESS.) 'Scuse me, where's the pay-phone?

WAITRESS: Sorry, we don't have a payph—

AL: Of *course* you don't have a payphone, of *course* you don't! Oh shit, let me outta here! (*Exits.*)

MARK: I don't know. It's not that bad in a Philadelphia.

WAITRESS: Could be worse. I've been in a Cleveland all week.

MARK: A Cleveland. What's that like?

WAITRESS: It's like death, without the advantages.

MARK: Really. Care to stand?

WAITRESS: Don't mind if I do. (*She sits.*)

MARK: I hope you won't reveal your name.

WAITRESS: Sharon.

MARK (*holds out his hand*): Good-bye.

WAITRESS: Hello. (*They shake.*)

MARK (*indicating the cheese steak*): Want to starve?

WAITRESS: Thanks. (*She picks up the cheese steak and starts eating.*)

MARK: Yeah, everybody has to be someplace. . . . (*Leans across the table with a smile.*) So.

BLACKOUT

LONG AGO

AND

FAR AWAY

A WINTER'S TALE

Nessun maggior dolore
che ricordarsi del tempo felice
ne la miseria; a cio sà 'l tuo dottore.

Ma s'a conoscer la prima radice
del nostro amor tu hai cotanto affetto,
dirò come colui che piange e dice.

Dante, *Inferno*
Canto V

This play is for
Lisa Schwarzbaum

Long Ago and Far Away was first presented at the Ensemble Studio Theatre in New York City in May 1993. It was directed by Christopher A. Smith; the set design was by H. Peet Foster; costume design was by Julie Doyle; lighting design was by Greg MacPherson. The cast was as follows:

LAURA	Crista Moore
GUS	John Ottavino
JACK	Baxter Harris
LANDLADY	Gretchen Walther

The main room of an apartment in New York City. Except for a few boxes and a CD player against the wall, the place is empty. There is a fireplace without a fire in it, a door to the outside at left, and an open doorway to a hallway at center. LAURA, *thirty and handsome, is sitting on a packing box and looking at a pen which she holds in her hand, turning it over and over. After a moment,* GUS, *same age, enters from center carrying a box.*

GUS: This is the end of it. Nine pounds of ancient correspondence. (LAURA *says nothing.*) Aloha.

LAURA: I'm sorry.

GUS: Lost in space?

LAURA: Yeah, I was, a little.

GUS: You're probably exhausted.

LAURA: No, I'm good. I'm *very* good.

GUS: Good. Excellent. (*Kisses her.*) Happy day, happy day, happy day. And this is just the prequel. (*He notices an old record album lying on a crate near* LAURA.) What's this?

LAURA: I don't know. I found it when I was cleaning.

GUS: "Long Ago and Far Away and Other Favorite Songs." Looks ancient. (*Holds it to his ear. Timex commercial.*) "But it's *still ticking!*" Yours?

LAURA: No, I've never seen it before.

GUS: A mysterious object. (*Noting a newspaper.*) Did you see us in the *Times* today?

LAURA: We were in the *Times*?

GUS: "West Nineties apartment near Central Park. Brownstone building. One bedroom, small study, remodelled kitchen, marble fireplace." Of course, they didn't mention that the fireplace doesn't *work*, but . . .

LAURA: How do you know it was us?

GUS: Well. West Nineties. Near Park. Fireplace. Sounded like us. And a million other apartments, it's true. But somehow I had this weird feeling they were talking about us.

LAURA: A woman disappeared.

GUS: A woman what . . . ?

LAURA: Did you see that in the paper? A woman in our neighborhood disappeared.

GUS: New neighborhood or old neighborhood?

LAURA: This neighborhood.

GUS: Anybody we know? We'll take her off the Rolodex.

LAURA: Ruth somebody.

GUS: Ah. Ruth Somebody. *Her.*

LAURA: Her husband came home and pots were cooking on the stove, the TV was on, all her clothes were still in the closet—and she was gone.

GUS: Still more reasons to move. Can't live in a neighborhood where you have people just *disappearing* on you.

LAURA: "Vanished without a trace . . ."

GUS: She probably ran off with a Hindu ski instructor. Got caught in a time warp, or an alternative reality. Anyway, she'll be back. Even in a separate reality you need a change of socks.

LAURA: A couple of years from now we'll probably see her picture in the paper and they'll say she's never been heard from.

GUS: Mmm. Husband heartbroken. Friends and neighbors baffled. "Ruth was always such a *wonderful* person."

LAURA: She has to be somewhere. Even if you disappear you don't just . . . disappear.

GUS: You're in a pretty spooky mood tonight. Care for a final celebratory glass of wine at the old homestead?

LAURA: Sure.

GUS: Mmm. Not the most convincing reading of that line I've ever heard.

LAURA: Yes, please. I'd love some wine.

GUS: Brilliant. (*Kisses her.*) Are you sure you're okay?

LAURA: Yeah. Fine.

GUS (*pouring wine*): Did these people say when they were coming over? The phantom apartment-seekers?

LAURA: No, just tonight sometime.

GUS: I don't see why we have to hang around for them. I told Tony and Bea we'd go out and celebrate. The really meaningful question for tonight being, do we go to the Empire Pagoda for their incomparable cold sesame noodles, to the Empire Dragon for the superb eggplant with garlic sauce, or to the Empire Valley for the killer Moo Shoo pork. Someplace conducive to dissecting this latest spate of bad movies—including that Lithuanian ode to ennui they sent us to. You're absolutely sure you're all right?

LAURA: I'm splendid.

GUS: I've always said so. (*Hands her a glass of wine.*) Cheers, babe. To better days.

LAURA: Why "*better* days"?

GUS: Well. The new apartment. The great future out there ahead of us. The fact that I got insulted in the street today. Days have got to get better than that.

LAURA: You got insulted . . . ?

GUS: *Still* more reasons to move.

LAURA: On our street?

GUS: Today. And I don't even . . . Maybe this was a metaphysical experience. Maybe I hallucinated it. Who knows. Anyway I'm coming up the street and up ahead of me I see this couple sitting on a doorstep about halfway down the block. A man and a woman.

LAURA: Homeless people?

GUS: Just ordinary everyday-looking people. Ergo, probably homeless. Anyway, the guy looks over and sees me coming and he nudges the woman and she looks over at me so all the time I'm walking by them I can feel them *looking* at me. You know? All this while still saying nothing. So I sail on and I'm probably about two feet past them when I hear the guy turn to the woman—obviously talking about me—and he says to her (*with a smirk*) *"See what I mean?"*

LAURA: "See what I . . . "?

GUS: "See what I mean?" What the hell is *that* supposed to mean? I never see these people before in my life, then I go walking by and—"See what I mean?" They had to be talking about me. And if I'm the punch line to somebody's story, I'd kind of like to know what the joke is! Is that insulting or what? And most insulting because I don't even know what it means! Any wisdom? Speculation? Thoughts?

LAURA: Do you know what I think I've just realized?

GUS: You were the woman on the doorstep? No. Tell me.

LAURA: I think I've only just realized that this is reality.

GUS: Excuse me? Did you just say "This is reality"?

LAURA: I think I've just realized that I exist.

GUS: You mean, tonight, or . . . ?

LAURA: No, I mean . . . Lately so often it's like there are these . . . moments of illumination . . .

GUS: Hmmmmmmmmmmmm.

LAURA: . . . when just for a second or two I realize, I mean I *really* realize, that this—all this—is really here. That it exists. And that I'm part of it. I don't know. Somehow it just recently hit me that when philosophers talk about the nature of reality, they're not talking about words, or ideas, they're talking about things like this box, and this newspaper, and this pen in my hand. Which are all *real*.

GUS: Uh-huh.

LAURA: I am *in* the universe. It's so strange. There's this large empty hole a billion years old and a trillion light years across, and I'm standing on a tiny piece of a small rock flying through it. We are. Everybody is. Right now. At this instant. I exist, and this pen exists. It's sitting in my hand. In my living hand . . .

GUS: Uh-huh. Listen, just click the heels of your ruby slippers together and say "There's no place like home, there's no place like home. . . . "

LAURA: Oh go to hell.

GUS: Go to hell? Come on, Laura. "This is reality"?! This is New York. This is hell. *This Is Your Life* with Ralph Edwards, maybe. But—"this is *reality*?" "I am in the universe"? Okay. I'm sorry. I didn't mean to not take you seriously.

LAURA: Nice job, buddy.

GUS: It's just—When somebody says "This is reality," anything you say in response is bound to sound a little trite. What *is* the proper riposte to "This is reality"?

LAURA: Why does everything have to be a riposte? Why does everything have to be a snappy answer?

GUS: Well. A little snap takes the sting out of reality. This being the *only* reality. And I've known *you* to snap out an answer in your time. The original riposte-woman. Even though tonight you're impersonating Hamlet the melancholy dame. But listen, if you want to take up philosophy, sort of a thoughtful hobby on top of an already lucrative career, I say go for it. I'll back you up, honey.

LAURA: Okay, okay. I was being trite. So shoot me.

GUS: I can't shoot you. You wouldn't exist anymore, and what would I do with all the furniture? We finally get a bigger apartment and she dies on me! Oh great! Thanks very much!

LAURA: But you know what?

GUS: What.

LAURA: This pen still exists in my hand.

GUS AND LAURA: *In my living hand.*

LAURA: Thank you.

GUS: Maybe we could sell this to Parker Pens. "The new bottom-line fountain pen. Doesn't write very well—but it exists."

LAURA: "To Bic or not to Bic."

GUS: That's the spirit. You know what you need in your present mood? You need my new invention. Listen to this, you'll love it. *Two-D glasses.* You put them on and everything looks like a movie. Is that brilliant? Those days when the shit is hitting the fan at the speed of light, you just pop these on and, Hey, no problem! I'm in a movie! Available in black-and-white, or technicolor for that gaudy MGM look. Perfect for somebody with reality jitters like yourself. What's the matter?

LAURA: Nothing.

GUS: Here's a philosophical speculation. Since you're in a philosophical mood. You know how the secret purpose of bees is to pollinate flowers? Has anybody ever thought the secret purpose of human beings might be to pollinate furniture? I mean look. I sit down on a couch, I move to a dining-room chair, carrying some couch pollen on the backs of my thighs, maybe in the middle of the night a little divan quietly blossoms into being. Or maybe I sit in a chair, you sit in a chair, we change chairs, and a love seat is born.

LAURA: Could you be quiet for a minute? Please?

GUS: I'm sorry. Was I babbling again?

LAURA: I'm sorry.

GUS: Well. You're in a rather somber and serious mood and I was feeling rather good. Just wanted to keep things lively.

LAURA: Don't you sometimes . . .

GUS: What.

LAURA: Sometimes I think I live in the world but I don't know anything about it. Even after all these years. I still don't know the first thing about the world. I don't know anything about anything! Lately some days I think my life's just going to go on and on like this. And then stop.

GUS: Go on like what?

LAURA: Well. Like this.

GUS: What's "this"? And what's wrong with "this"?

LAURA: No—nothing. I just . . .

GUS: We're doing great.

LAURA: Sure.

GUS: As always.

LAURA: We're doing fine.

GUS: Mmm. Not the most convincing reading of that line I've ever heard.

LAURA: You yourself said "to *better* days."

GUS: Oh come on, Laura.

LAURA: Implying that everything isn't as perfect as it could be.

GUS: I just meant—I didn't mean anything, I just . . .

LAURA: It's like tonight. We'll go out with Tony and Bea and we'll argue about which restaurant to go to—as if it was important—and then we'll talk about what movies we've all seen and we'll all be very clever and have a lot of snappy answers and then we'll discuss and compare the food we're eating and the food we've had this week and the food we're planning to eat and the movie reviews in the *Times,* and then we'll go home and everything will be the same as it was until the next time we meet to talk about restaurants and movies.

GUS: Well. There's nothing wrong per se with restaurants and movies. I mean, Szechwan cooking and bad foreign films are what make life worth living.

LAURA: Mm.

GUS: Laura, what is with you tonight? You're a dirge. You're the Brahms *German Requiem* when you ought to be a Rodgers and Hammerstein musical. We're moving out! This is no time for philosophy! I have seen the future and it's Riverside Drive! And it is going to be great!

LAURA: What if they never find that woman?

GUS: What?

LAURA: This Ruth. What if it's never explained what happened to her? And she really does vanish without a trace?

GUS: Help me out here. I think I missed a chapter.

LAURA: Gus, maybe we shouldn't move.

GUS: Shouldn't *move*? Wait a minute, Laura. Pump the brake slowly, we're sliding.

LAURA: We've been in this place a long time. We like this place.

GUS: We're moving. Okay? No. We have *moved*.

LAURA: Why should we move?

GUS: First of all we haven't been in this place all that long.

LAURA: We've been here long enough.

GUS: And it's always been too small. What about when little feet are pattering all around us? We'll need a lot more room then, whenever that happens, which as far as I understand we both hope will be relatively soon. Or am I right?

LAURA: But this place—

GUS: Yes. This place is us. This place will always be us and all the good times "us" have had here. We've also just spent a huge amount of time and trouble finding a *new* place that we like and can afford, and . . . I don't think you have reality jitters. You have moving panic. You know. That weird disjointed melancholy that settles over you right before you leave a place where you've been happy? But you can be happy in another place!

LAURA: Have you really been happy here?

GUS: Yes! I've been very happy here.

LAURA: Are you happy now?

GUS: Well no, not right *now*, right now I'm talking rather loudly trying to remind you that this is us, here. Remember? Us?

LAURA: And what is that?

GUS: You are going off your head, woman. And you're very quickly sending me off of mine.

LAURA: The night my father died . . . And this was after they gave up hope on him and he knew he didn't have much time . . . The night before he died he got into this . . . panic, he started thrashing around in the bed and telling my mother to call the doctor. And all this time my mother sat there by the bed holding his hand and saying, "The doctor can't help you, Bill. The doctor can't help you anymore."

GUS: Laura, what can I do for you?

LAURA: Nothing.

GUS: Talk to me. What can I do?

LAURA: My father died this miserable ugly death screaming for a doctor and then vanished without a trace.

GUS: He didn't *vanish*, he . . .

LAURA: My mother vanished. You and I will vanish too, along with a billion other people. Without a ripple.

GUS: Where did this cheery mood come from, anyway?

LAURA: Some days it's like my life is made of this incredibly thin white tissue, it's like a wall of very fine gauze. And the events from somebody's life are being projected on that fabric—and it's my life. Woman brushing her teeth. Woman sitting at her desk. And this membrane is so thin, it's like I could reach out and just push my finger right through it.

GUS: I don't know what to tell you.

LAURA: And what would I see if I could push through that fabric? What would I see on the other side?

GUS: I don't know. Probably New Jersey.

LAURA: Then I think—no. This is reality.

GUS: You know maybe you *do* need 2-D glasses. You're halfway there already. In your case, maybe 1-D glasses—

LAURA: Jesus Christ, Gus!

GUS: I'm sorry, I just . . . I'm trying to deal here. Laura, this is a mood, it's . . . Nothing is different! We're the same people we were yesterday. You're just . . .

LAURA: All my life—I guess I've just realized this too—all my life I've somehow taken it for granted that everything would be explained someday. Like I'd get to the last chapter and I'd find out who the killer was, a messenger would arrive and explain why this happened to me when I was twelve, or whatever happened to some . . . book I lost when I was fifteen, and what this all meant. But that's never going to happen. You don't find these things out. You never find anything out.

GUS: Yes. Life is a mystery. That's very profound.

LAURA: Fuck you.

GUS: Fuck me? First go to hell, now fuck you. All in one night. Okay.

LAURA: *Fuck you.*

GUS: Laura, what the hell am I supposed to tell you? That everything *will* be explained someday? An angel's going to come down and hand you the winning envelope with the secret of life in it? I don't think that's going to happen. Or—okay—it *won't* be explained. I agree with you. We don't know anything about anything. We're idiots in a dark and mysterious universe. Does that make you feel better? Now what do you say we head over to Tony and Bea's and we won't talk about restaurants or movies. We'll talk about whatever you want. We'll talk philosophy.

LAURA: This is not . . .

GUS: Okay.

LAURA: This is not philosophy, Gus. This is not a *mood*.

GUS: Okay.

LAURA: This is my life.

GUS: Yes.

LAURA: This is my life.

GUS: And what can I do for you, to make your life better?

LAURA: I just keep hearing my mother say that. "The doctor can't help you, Bill. The doctor can't help you anymore."

GUS: Well. I will not be brought down. I refuse to be brought down. I was feeling so . . . good, I . . . How can I convince you that everything is good, that your life is good, that your life isn't any worse or different than it was yesterday?

LAURA: Why don't you go and I'll wait for these people.

GUS: Forget these people! Fuck 'em!

LAURA: I'll finish packing. You go on.

GUS: Okay. You finish packing.

LAURA: I'm not that hungry anyway.

GUS: Okay.

LAURA: I'm lousy company tonight.

GUS: Well. There's the CD player needs to be packed. You could tape up these boxes. (*He puts on his coat.*) I'll call you before we go anywhere and tell you where we're going. In case you hear the call of Chow Fun. What's the matter now?

LAURA: I just thought, you wouldn't have done this when we first met. Or even a year ago.

GUS: What.

LAURA: You would've stayed here and waited with me.

GUS: I didn't mean to— I just wanted to— Oh, JESUS!

LAURA: And I'm not saying that to accuse you, I just—

GUS: What is that, a form of praise? A term of endearment? "You wouldn't have done that when we first met"?

LAURA: I'm saying things change. Things were better.

GUS: When?

LAURA: Better days.

GUS: You set me up, Laura.

LAURA: I didn't set you up.

GUS: You offered to stay and then you accuse me of abandoning you. I think that's pretty fucking mean.

LAURA: That's not what I mean.

GUS: Well maybe someday I'll get an explanation of what you mean. When I reach the last chapter and everything's explained. When the fucking messenger arrives. (*She says nothing.*) Okay. I'm going over there. I'll call you in a while.

LAURA: 'Bye.

GUS: I think— Oh fuck it. We'll talk later. (*He exits left.*)

(LAURA *sits on the box again and puts her face into her hands for a moment. Then she goes to the CD player against the wall and turns it on. Music comes on, softly. There is a knock at the door left.*)

LAURA: Gus—? (LAURA *opens the door to* JACK, *sixty, in a long, shabby coat with snowflakes on the shoulders.*) Oh. Hi. Sorry. I thought you were my husband.

JACK: I was just wondering if I could look at your apartment.

LAURA: Sure. Absolutely. Come on in. (JACK *hesitates.*) Really. Come in.

(JACK *comes in.*)

JACK: I'm sorry to bother you.

LAURA: No. No bother. I knew you were coming sometime
tonight.

JACK: You knew I was coming . . . ?

LAURA: The agent told us. I'm Laura. And—I'm sorry—your
name is . . . ?

JACK: Jack.

LAURA: Hello, Jack. (*Jack looks around himself in silence for a moment.*) Is it snowing out now? Looks like you've got snow
on your coat. (*No response.*) Jack . . . ?

JACK: Yes. It's snowing out. (*He keeps looking about at the room.*)

LAURA: You know, somehow I thought there were going to be
two of you. I mean, I thought they said a husband and wife.

JACK: No. It's just me.

LAURA: Uh-huh. Well. This is the place. Living room. Obviously. Fireplace. Which doesn't work, unfortunately.
Though some of the shutters still work. Then there's a bedroom and a small study down the hall, and a kitchen and
bathroom off to the left. (JACK *is standing in the center of the
room, very still, with his eyes closed.*) And that's pretty much it.
If you want to take a look.

JACK: God. God.

(LAURA *takes this in for a moment.*)

LAURA: You know, the rent is pretty steep. I don't know if they
made that clear. (JACK *says nothing, remaining perfectly still.*)
By the way—how did you get into the building? I mean it's
a pretty safe building, usually you have to buzz people in.

JACK: The fireplace doesn't work?

LAURA: Contrary to the ad. It did once. (JACK *says nothing.*) But listen, Jack. I do have lots of things to do, we're right in the middle of packing here, so I'm afraid I'm going to have to let you go soon. My husband'll be coming back in a second. And we can't go on meeting like this.

JACK: Fuck. Fuck. Fuck. Fuck.

LAURA: Jack, you're going to have to go now. I don't want to have to call somebody.

JACK: The fireplace used to work. And all the shutters. (*Indicating the wall at right.*) This was a doorway into the kitchen, right here. Just a tiny little . . . You couldn't open the refrigerator and stand in the kitchen at the same time.

LAURA: So you used to live here, once upon a time.

JACK (*indicating the doorway, center*): This was a bathroom, through here. With a beautiful bright red door. Very red.

LAURA: Taking a trip down memory lane tonight, huh?

JACK: And this was the whole place. There weren't any other rooms. This was it. And it seemed enormous. (*Pointing to where they'd been.*) Couch. Chair. Rug over there, Turkish rug. Table. Books. Books. And the bed, over here. (*He goes to far left.*) This was where we used to make love. Right on this spot. Right here. Right . . . here. Nights like this we'd build a fire and close up the shutters. Take our clothes off. Drink wine and talk philosophy all night in bed. The meaning of life. Do you understand? The meaning of life.

LAURA: Yes.

JACK: She found this old record here somebody'd left behind. We'd play it over and over and over again.

LAURA: "Long Ago and Far Away."

JACK: "Long Ago and Far Away." There was the whole rest of the universe and this one little place, and the two of us inside it. Warming our hands at each other. Everything led right here, to this room and the two of us. Talking, talking, talking.

LAURA: About the meaning of life.

JACK: It was paradise.

LAURA: And she——? Where is she?

JACK: Paradise . . .

(*Thoughtful now,* LAURA *doesn't notice as* JACK *goes out through the doorway at center—where a bright red door appears, quietly closing shut. The music on the CD player fades out, and we hear an old recording of "Long Ago and Far Away." The CD player goes into the wall and is replaced by an old phonograph.* LAURA *notices this and turns as a fire blazes up in the fireplace, and the wall at right opens, revealing a tiny kitchen. As* LAURA *stands there looking at all this, the door left opens and a* LANDLADY *steps in.*)

LANDLADY: What's going on here? (*She goes to the record player and turns it off.*) How did you get in here?

LAURA: Well I . . .

LANDLADY: I didn't hear the doorbell. Who let you in?

LAURA: Nobody. I was here.

LANDLADY: You were here. And the fire? That started itself?

LAURA: It did, actually.

LANDLADY: Mm-hm. I suppose you're the one looking for the room.

LAURA: Excuse me?

LANDLADY: Are you here to look at the room? Well?

LAURA: Um. Yes. I'm here to look at the room.

LANDLADY: Well. This is the room. Sorry about the mess. The last tenants left all this behind. (*She indicates the boxes.*)

LAURA: I don't understand. . . .

LANDLADY: The people who lived here before left these things.

LAURA: No, I understand that, but—

LANDLADY: It's a single-room studio apartment. Bathroom's through there. You got new plumbing and a new toilet and sink. You can see the kitchen through there. It's small, but everything works. I pay heat and water, you pay electric, rent is eighty dollars a month payable on the first. If you're interested, I can give you an application. I suppose you have references?

LAURA: References. . . .

LANDLADY: Do you have a job? Are you working?

LAURA: I did have a job. I'm not sure I have it anymore.

LANDLADY: So you're out of work.

LAURA: Well. I don't really know. (*Off her look.*) I'm not crazy.

LANDLADY: It's always the crazy ones who say that. I see a ring there on your finger. This means you're married?

LAURA: I have been married.

LANDLADY: So where's your husband?

LAURA: My husband sort of . . . disappeared.

LANDLADY: Mm. You got any kids, or . . . ?

LAURA: No. No kids.

LANDLADY: So you're just looking for yourself.

LAURA: Listen, do you mind if I just sit here for a minute? And think about all this?

LANDLADY: I got some others coming to look, so if you want the room you'd better say so. I can't promise anything. And I can't wait forever. (*She starts out.*)

LAURA: Yes.

LANDLADY: Yes what.

LAURA: I want the room. I'll take it.

LANDLADY: You'll take the room. Just like that.

LAURA: Well. I think I could be very happy here. The shutters work, don't they?

LANDLADY: The shutters work. Everything.

LAURA: I could put a couch here. A chair here. Turkish rug. Bed over here . . . Who knows. It could be paradise.

LANDLADY: I'm going to need something in advance, if you don't have a job.

LAURA: I can find a job. Really.

LANDLADY: Well . . .

LAURA: I'm a very good tenant.

LANDLADY: Why don't I get an application and we'll talk about it. And your name is—?

LAURA: My name is Ruth.

LANDLADY: Ruth. (*The* LANDLADY *goes out up left.* LAURA *looks around at the place.*)

LAURA: Yes, I think I could be very happy here. . . . (*She sees her wine glass, still half-full, sitting on the mantel. She picks it up, turns the record player back on, and "Long Ago and Far Away" comes back on. She carries the wine glass into the kitchen, and suddenly the wall closes up behind her. The red door disappears at center, the open doorway reappears, and the fire goes out in the fireplace. The record player is replaced by the CD player as the song fades out and the other music returns. The door left opens and* GUS *comes in.*)

GUS: Laura, look, I'm sorry— (*He sees that she's not there.*) Laura . . . ? (JACK *enters from center.*) Who're you? Are you the, to look at the apartment? I'm looking for my wife. Is she back there? Laura . . . ? (GUS *goes out at center, and we hear him offstage.*) Laura . . . ? (JACK *stands at the place where the bed had been at far left. After a moment,* GUS *reenters.*) Where is she? Did she go out, or . . . ?

JACK: Would you take this? (*He hands* GUS *a white envelope.*) Give it to somebody?

GUS: What is this . . . ?

JACK: That'll explain everything.

GUS: The fuck is going on around here . . . ?

(JACK *has taken a pistol out of his coat. He puts the gun to his heart and fires. He falls.* GUS *backs off in shock, looking down at the body.*)

Jesus. Jesus . . . *Laura?!*

(*Nothing. He drops down onto the box where* LAURA *was sitting at the beginning.*)

BLACKOUT

FOREPLAY,

OR

THE ART OF

THE FUGUE

*This play is for
Bennett Cohen*

Foreplay, or The Art of the Fugue was first presented at the Manhattan Punch Line Theatre (Steve Kaplan, artistic director) in New York City in February 1991. It was directed by Jason McConnell Buzas; the set design was by Vaughn Patterson; costume design was by Kitty Leech; lighting design was by Pat Dignan. The cast was as follows:

AMY	Laura Dean
CHUCK	Robert Stanton
ANNIE	Alison Martin
CHUCK II	Tony Carlin
ALMA	Anne O'Sullivan
CHUCK III	Brian Howe

A bare stage representing a miniature-golf course. Upstage, a sign that says LILLI-PUTT LANE. *(Note: Actual golf balls are not used, though the motions are made of setting them down, putting, retrieving them from holes, etc.)* CHUCK *and* AMY *enter, with golf clubs. They are both in their early twenties.*

CHUCK: *Fore!*

AMY: I can't believe I'm out here.

CHUCK: Amy, you are going to fall in love tonight.

AMY: I am?

CHUCK: With miniature golf.

AMY: Chuck . . .

CHUCK: I swear. This night will turn you into a miniature-golf-o-*maniac.* You're going to like this game so much, you'll wake up shorter tomorrow.

AMY: Very cute.

CHUCK: Just remember one thing: miniature golf is bigger than you or me.

AMY *(setting a "ball" down)*: You must be some kind of a charmer, to talk me into this.

CHUCK: So take your best shot and just try to resist. Go on.

AMY: Okay . . .

CHUCK *(as she hits the ball)*: *Puck! (As it travels.)* Aaaaaaaaaaaaaa-aand— *(It misses.)* Ouch.

AMY: Ohhhhhhhhhhhh . . . *(This disappointed, fading moan is the sound that* AMY *will typically make when she misses a shot.)*

CHUCK: Too bad. Did you know, by the way, that a race of dwarves once covered the earth? This (*the miniature-golf course*) is what they left behind.

AMY: Ha, ha.

CHUCK: This was their Stonehenge. Castle. Windmill. Lighthouse.

AMY: Did you just think of this?

CHUCK: You didn't know that but it's true.

AMY: Did you just make that up?

CHUCK (*motioning for her to proceed*): But please.

AMY: I don't know how I got into this.

CHUCK (*as she putts again*): *Puck!* Aaaaaaaaaaaand—*Ouch.*

AMY (*missing*): Ohhhhhhhhhh . . .

CHUCK: Nice bounce. But no cigar.

AMY: It wasn't a *bad* shot.

CHUCK: Anyway, that's why I come out here to Lilli-Putt Lane. To sense a cosmic connection with the ancient anthropology of the game.

AMY: Uh-huh. And to seduce girls.

CHUCK: *What?!*

AMY: Oh come on, Chuck.

CHUCK: What guy in his right mind would take a girl miniature-*golfing* to seduce her?

AMY: You would. You've got quite a reputation, you know.

CHUCK: What "reputation"?

AMY: *Don Juan.*

CHUCK: Amy, I swear. I've never taken a girl miniature-golfing in my life. Or anybody *else's* life!

AMY: Uh-huh.

CHUCK: But do you want to take your next shot? I can see you're getting hooked.

AMY (*lining up the putt*): If this is about getting into bed with me . . .

CHUCK: Never in a million years.

AMY: You can think again.

CHUCK (*as she putts*): *Puck!* Aaaaaaaaaaaaaaaaaand—

AMY (*as it goes in*): *Yes!*

CHUCK: *Hey!* That was good, Amy!

AMY: That was good, wasn't it?

CHUCK: That was *very* good.

AMY: Wow! That felt *great!*

CHUCK: It's almost an erotic thrill, isn't it? (*Off her look.*) I take it back. It's not an erotic thrill. It's a mild celibate *frisson.*

AMY: You are shameless.

CHUCK (*getting ready to putt*): Quiet, please. I'm concentrating here. (*He tees off.*) *Puck!*

AMY (*as the ball travels*): Mmmmmmmmmmmmmmmmmmmmmm!

CHUCK (*overlapping that*): Aaaaaaaaaaaaaaaaaaaaaaaand . . . (*The ball goes in.*) BINGO!

AMY: Wow!

CHUCK: Am I good?

AMY: That was *nice!*

CHUCK: Am I good?

AMY: You're really good.

CHUCK: Okay. Let's put this down for infinity. (*Marks a score-card.*) Three for Amy. And a hole in one for Chuck.

AMY: God. It takes so little, doesn't it.

CHUCK: So little?

AMY: To make people happy. It takes so little for happiness.

CHUCK: And what's littler than miniature golf? So are you getting interested? Shall we play on?

AMY: Yeah. Let's play on.

CHUCK: *FORE!*

CHUCK II (*offstage*): *FORE!*

(*As* CHUCK *and* AMY *move on to the second hole,* CHUCK II *enters with* ANNIE *at the first hole.* CHUCK II *is dressed exactly like* CHUCK. ANNIE *is in her mid-twenties.*)

ANNIE: Chuck, they ought to lock you up.

CHUCK II: What . . . ?

ANNIE: You are *shameless*, Chuck.

CHUCK: This is nothing, you know.

AMY: What.

CHUCK II: Annie, *what*?

CHUCK: I once played miniature golf in Japan.

AMY: In Japan?

ANNIE: Oh, right.

CHUCK: Right there on the slopes of Mount Fuji.

CHUCK II: I've never taken a girl miniature-golfing in my entire life!

ANNIE: I'll bet.

CHUCK II: I swear!

CHUCK: I swear!

CHUCK II: Or anybody *else's* entire life!

AMY AND ANNIE: Uh-huh.

CHUCK II: You don't believe me?

ANNIE: With your reputation?

CHUCK II: What reputation?

ANNIE: *Don Juan*.

CHUCK II: Oh Amy, Amy. You have to learn to trust people.

CHUCK (*as* AMY *gets ready to tee off again*): Trust yourself, now.

ANNIE: Annie.

CHUCK II: Excuse me?

ANNIE: My name is Annie. You called me Amy.

CHUCK II: I'm sorry. *Annie*.

ANNIE (*sets her "ball" down*): I'm going to keep my eye on you.

CHUCK (*to* AMY): Just keep your eye on the ball.

CHUCK II: Annie-way—prepare to fall in love tonight. With miniature golf.

ANNIE: Oh yes?

CHUCK II: This game is bigger than you or me, you know.

ANNIE: Very clever. I just hope nobody *sees* me out here.

CHUCK AND CHUCK II (*as* AMY *and* ANNIE *tee off*): *Puck!*

CHUCK II: Aaaaaaaaand . . .

CHUCK: Aaaaaaaaaaaaaand . . .

AMY: Mmmmmmmmmmmmmmmmmmm . . .

ANNIE (*her typical sound, at missing a shot*): *Nyugh!*

AMY: Ohhhhhhhhhh . . .

CHUCK: Too bad.

CHUCK II: Nice lay, though.

CHUCK: Very nice lay.

CHUCK II (*off Annie's look*): It's just a *golfing* term.

CHUCK: It's perfectly innocent.

AMY AND ANNIE: I'm sure. (*The women get ready to putt again.*)

CHUCK: But you know in Japan, the people are so short, miniature golf is *really* miniature over there. Like this high. (*Ankle-height.*)

AMY: Very cute.

CHUCK: You didn't know that, but it's true.

CHUCK II: Did you know, by the way, that a race of dwarves once covered the earth? This is what they left behind.

ANNIE: Ha, ha.

CHUCK II: This was their Stonehenge.

ANNIE: Very cute.

CHUCK II: You didn't know that but it's true.

AMY: I know you're only trying to distract me.

ANNIE: You're not going to distract me.

CHUCK II: *Puck!*

CHUCK: *Puck!*

CHUCK AND CHUCK II: Aaaaaaaaaaaaand—

CHUCK II (*as* ANNIE *misses*): *BONG.*

ANNIE: *Nyugh!*

AMY: Ohhhhhhhhhhh . . .

CHUCK II: Anyway, that's why I come out here. To sense a cosmic connection with my shorter predecessors.

AMY: Did you just make all that up?

ANNIE: Does somebody write all this for you?

CHUCK AND CHUCK II: What?

AMY: Golfing in Japan.

CHUCK II: I don't make anything up.

CHUCK: This is truth!

ANNIE: You do have . . .

AMY: There is *something* about you . . .

ANNIE: Charm. I guess.

CHUCK II: I'm a very serious guy!

CHUCK: I'm a very serious guy, at heart.

AMY: You sure have a way of making everything mean something else.

CHUCK: And that's exactly what I like about miniature golf.

CHUCK II: Do you know what I like about this game?

CHUCK: It means something else.

CHUCK II: It's a metaphor.

CHUCK: It's a great metaphor.

ANNIE: Okay. A metaphor.

AMY AND ANNIE: What *for*?

AMY: *I* know.

ANNIE: For sex.

AMY: For seduction.

CHUCK: No—

CHUCK II: No—

ANNIE: Sure. "Keeping *score*."

AMY: "Getting it in the *hole*."

CHUCK: No—

CHUCK II: No—

CHUCK: No! It's a metaphor for *life*!

CHUCK II: For *death*.

ANNIE: Did you say "for *death*"?

CHUCK II: Those aren't just *holes* out there.

CHUCK: These are stages on the journey of life.

CHUCK II: The course always leads to the same final place.

CHUCK: But the course is different for everybody.

CHUCK II: Sand traps.

CHUCK: Water holes.

CHUCK II: The sands of time.

CHUCK: The oases of purification.

CHUCK II: The final hole.

CHUCK: The verdant fairways . . .

AMY: What a beautiful idea!

ANNIE: What a crock of manure!

CHUCK: And I believe it.

ANNIE: Right. The five stages of miniature golf: anger, denial, grief, blame—and a windmill.

CHUCK II: That's good, Amy.

CHUCK: You're a good person.

ANNIE: Annie.

CHUCK II: Annie.

CHUCK: Amy.

CHUCK II: Maybe you're afraid of the challenge of miniature golf.

ANNIE: I'm afraid of the challenge of miniature *men*.

CHUCK II: Ha!

CHUCK AND CHUCK II: Play on?

AMY: Yeah.

ANNIE: Definitely.

AMY AND ANNIE: Let's play on.

CHUCK II: Good.

CHUCK AND CHUCK II (*as the women putt*): *Puck!*

CHUCK: Aaaaaaaaand . . .

CHUCK II: Aaaaaaaaaaaaand . . .

AMY (*joining in, overlapping*): Mmmmmmmmmmmmmmmmmm!

ANNIE (*joining in, overlapping*): Uhhhhhhhhhhhhhhhhhhhhhhh!

AMY AND ANNIE: *YES!*

CHUCK II: Nice shot.

CHUCK: Nice shot.

AMY: Boy, that felt good!

ANNIE: Whoo!

AMY: Well!

ANNIE: Wow. Thought I wasn't up to it, huh.

CHUCK: I told you you'd like it.

CHUCK II: Maybe you only needed to . . . handle the equipment.

ANNIE: But the club is so small.

CHUCK II: Ha, ha.

ANNIE: Ho, ho.

AMY: It really *is* an erotic thrill, isn't it?

CHUCK II: Okay.

CHUCK: You want to see an erotic thrill?

CHUCK II: Watch this.

CHUCK AND CHUCK II (*as they tee off, a soft sexual moan*): Mmf. (*As the ball travels, the orgasm grows.*)

CHUCK: Oh, yes . . .

CHUCK II: Yes . . .

AMY: Mmmmmmmmmmmmmmm . . .

CHUCK: *Yes . . . !*

ANNIE: Ohhhhhhhhhh . . .

CHUCK II: YES!

CHUCK: YES!

AMY AND ANNIE: OHHHHHHHHHHHHH!

CHUCK II: *YES!*

CHUCK: *YES!*

CHUCK AND CHUCK II: *BINGO!* (*Collective fading postorgasmic moan.*)

AMY: Boy! Nice shot!

CHUCK: Am I good?

CHUCK II: Am I good?

ANNIE: You're good, all right.

AMY: You're very good.

CHUCK II: Okay. Let's put this down for infinity. (*The two* CHUCKS *mark their scorecards.*) A hole in one . . .

CHUCK: *Another* hole in one . . .

CHUCK AND CHUCK II: For Chuck.

CHUCK II: So are you enjoying yourself?

AMY: I'm having a very good time.

ANNIE: I *am* enjoying myself, in spite of myself.

CHUCK: Good.

CHUCK II: It takes so little, you know. To make people happy. Amy—

ANNIE: Annie.

CHUCK II: Annie . . .

CHUCK: Have you ever thought that there's a design in our lives?

CHUCK II: Maybe there's something bigger than all this.

ANNIE: Polo?

AMY: *I* think so.

CHUCK II: And you could be a part of it.

CHUCK: You could be a part of some greater design in my life.

CHUCK II: You're so different.

CHUCK: You're so different, somehow.

CHUCK II: You're not just . . . Annie-body.

ANNIE: Ha, ha.

CHUCK II: We could just forget golf, you know.

CHUCK: We could just go over to my place. The night is young.

CHUCK II: The stars are out. . . .

ANNIE: And chuck the game?

AMY: Why don't we see who wins first.

ANNIE: Let's play on a little.

CHUCK: Okay.

CHUCK AND CHUCK II: *FORE!*

CHUCK III (*offstage*): *FORE!*

(CHUCK III *enters with* ALMA.)

CHUCK III: Do you know I've never taken a girl miniature-golf-ing before?

ALMA: Oh yeah, how come? I been on lots of minichure-golf dates. (*That stops* CHUCK III *a little.*)

CHUCK III: Oh, really . . . ?

ALMA: Sure, I love minichure golf. I play it all the time.

CHUCK III (*not too heartily*): Well good . . .

CHUCK II: Did I tell you that I once played miniature golf in Japan?

ANNIE: In Japan?

CHUCK II: Yeah. Miniature golf is *really* miniature over there. (*Ankle-height.*)

ANNIE: Ha, ha.

CHUCK (*clearing his throat*): Hem, hem.

AMY: I know you're only trying to distract me.

CHUCK II: *Hem, hem.*

ANNIE: Very cute. May I play on now?

CHUCK II: Please.

CHUCK III: Did you know that a race of dwarves once covered the earth?

ALMA: They *DID*? *Dwarfs*?

CHUCK III: Well. Not really.

ALMA: You mean like *midgets*? Were all over the *world*?

CHUCK III: I was only kidding, actually.

ALMA: Oh boy, you had me scared! But I bet if that was true, they probably would've left something like this behind, huh? Like *Stonehenge* or something.

CHUCK III: Yeah.

ALMA: Wouldn't that be funny?

CHUCK III: Hysterical.

ANNIE: But why don't *you* go first.

AMY: *You* go first this time.

CHUCK: All right.

CHUCK II: Gladly.

ALMA: You want to go first?

CHUCK III: Be my guest. But just remember: this game is bigger than either one of us.

ALMA: Huh?

CHUCK III: It's *bigger* than us. *Bigger . . . ?*

ALMA: Oh. "Bigger" than us.

CHUCK III: Than us. Just a little joke. (CHUCK, CHUCK II, *and* ALMA *line up to tee off.*)

AMY (*clearing her throat*): Hem.

ANNIE (*clearing her throat*): Hem.

CHUCK II: That's not going to work, you know.

AMY (*as* CHUCK *putts*): *Puck!*

ANNIE (*as* CHUCK II *putts*): *Puck!*

CHUCK III (*as* ALMA *putts*): *Puck!*

CHUCKS I, II, AND III: Aaaaaaaaaaaaaaand . . .

CHUCK (*misses*): *Oof.*

CHUCK II (*misses*): Ouch.

AMY AND ANNIE: *BONG.*

ALMA: *YES! A HOLE IN ONE!*

ANNIE: Too bad.

AMY: Nice try, though.

ALMA: Was that good?

CHUCK III: That was good, Amy.

ALMA: Alma.

CHUCK III: Huh?

ALMA: My name is Alma, you called me Amy.

CHUCK III: Oh. Sorry.

ALMA: No problem. You want to shoot?

AMY AND ANNIE (*as* CHUCK *and* CHUCK II *putt again*): *Puck!*

CHUCK AND CHUCK II: Aaaaaaaaaaaaaaand . . .

CHUCK III: You know what I like about miniature golf?

ALMA: The metaphor?

AMY AND ANNIE: *BONG.*

ANNIE: Too bad.

ALMA: Do you like the life metaphor or the death metaphor?

CHUCK III: Uh—well. Never mind.

AMY: Nice try.

CHUCK III: It's not important.

ALMA: I just like this 'cause it's fun. Like sex or something. You want to . . . shoot?

CHUCK III: Sure.

ANNIE (*as* CHUCK II *putts*): *Puck!*

AMY (*as* CHUCK *putts*): *Puck!*

CHUCK III (*putting*): *Puck!*

CHUCK (*dully*): And—

CHUCK II (*not much verve*): Bingo. (ALMA *does a raspberry.*)

AMY: I wouldn't worry about it.

ANNIE: You're right on par for the hole. (AMY, ANNIE, *and* CHUCK III *get ready to putt.*)

ALMA: You've got quite a reputation, you know.

CHUCK III: Who, me?

ALMA: Yeah. As a Donald Juan.

CHUCK III: Oh. A Donald Juan.

ALMA: But you're gripping it wrong.

CHUCK III: Excuse me?

ALMA: Keep your thumbs down.

CHUCK III: Oh. Thanks.

CHUCK (*as* AMY *putts*): *Puck.*

AMY: *Yes!*

CHUCK II (*as* ANNIE *putts*): *Puck.*

ANNIE: Excellent!

CHUCK III (*as he putts*): *Puck.*

ALMA: (*Raspberry.*) Lousy lay, too. That's a golfing term.

ANNIE AND AMY: Scorecard, please. (CHUCK *and* CHUCK II *hand over their scorecards.*)

CHUCK III: You know I once played miniature golf in Japan?

ALMA: Must be pretty minichure, the people are so short.

CHUCK III: We haven't gone out *before*, have we?

ALMA: No.

CHUCK III: I mean, we haven't played this course before, have we?

ALMA: I don't think so.

AMY AND ANNIE : FORE!

CHUCK: So anyway.

CHUCK II: What's your story, Annie?

CHUCK: What's your background?

CHUCK III: Got any family?

AMY: I have two brothers.

ANNIE: Three sisters.

ALMA: Two brothers, a sister, a step-sister, a half-brother, and my dog Barky.

CHUCKS I, II, AND III: Uh-huh.

CHUCK (*as he putts*): *Puck.*

CHUCK II (*as he putts*): *Puck.*

CHUCK III (*as he putts*): *Puck.*

ALMA: Do you have to make those noises?

CHUCK: *Ouch.*

CHUCK II: *Oof.*

AMY AND ANNIE: *BONG.*

CHUCK III: What noises?

ALMA: You make noises while you golf.

CHUCK III: Oh. Sorry.

ALMA: Your shot again, Dick.

CHUCK III: It's *Chuck.*

ALMA: Oh. Sorry. (CHUCKS I, II, *and* III *prepare to putt again.*)

AMY: Anyway . . .

ANNIE: My mother's dead.

AMY: My father lives in Arkansas.

ALMA: My brother is an undertaker.

CHUCK AND CHUCK II: *Puck!*

AMY AND ANNIE: Aaaaaaaaaaaaaand—

ALMA: My sister is a dyke.

AMY AND ANNIE: *BONG!*

ALMA (*as* CHUCK III *misses*): (*Raspberry.*)

CHUCK III: You know, *you* make noises too.

ALMA: I do?

CHUCK III: Oh yeah.

ALMA: Funny. *I* never noticed.

CHUCK II: So this brother . . .

CHUCK: How old is your sister?

ANNIE: I don't have a brother.

AMY: It's two brothers.

CHUCK III: So your mother is dead?

ALMA: No, she's a beautician.

CHUCK: But your father is a carpenter?

CHUCK II: Your mother lives in Michigan?

CHUCK III: And you're divorced?

AMY, ANNIE, AND ALMA: No!

AMY: He's a pickle packer.

ANNIE: Buried in Kansas.

ALMA: But I do have a boyfriend in the Navy.

CHUCKS I, II, AND III: Oh. (*The three* CHUCKS *putt.*)

AMY AND ANNIE: *Puck!*

CHUCK AND CHUCK II: Aaaaaaaaaaaaand—!

AMY, ANNIE, CHUCKS I AND II: BINGO!

ALMA: (*Raspberry.*)

CHUCK III: You know I can't hit the ball if I don't go *"puck."*

ALMA: *"Puck"?*

CHUCK III: I have to make a noise if I'm going to hit it right.

ALMA: Oh. Okay. Make a noise.

CHUCK III: It's my nature.

ALMA: Okay.

CHUCK III: I'm used to it.

ALMA: Go ahead. Make all the noise you want.

CHUCK (*referring to* CHUCK III): Looks like we've got a real moron up ahead here.

CHUCK III (*feeling* ALMA *watching him*): You're not going to make me miss my shot.

ALMA: It's two inches away! Just hit it!

CHUCK AND CHUCK II: *Playing through!*

CHUCK III: *Puck.*

CHUCK AND CHUCK II: *Playing through!*

CHUCK III: And bingo.

AMY: Okay, now.

ANNIE: This is *war.*

CHUCK AND CHUCK II, AMY, ANNIE (*as* AMY *and* ANNIE *putt*): *Puck!*

CHUCK AND CHUCK II: Aaaaaaaaaaaaand . . .

AMY AND ANNIE: All right!

CHUCK AND CHUCK II, AMY, ANNIE (*as* CHUCK, CHUCK II, *and* ALMA *putt*): *Puck!*

AMY AND ANNIE: Aaaaaaaaaaaaaaand . . .

CHUCK AND CHUCK II: BINGO!

ALMA: *Yes! ANOTHER HOLE IN ONE!* Want to shoot?

CHUCK AND AMY: *Puck!*

AMY: Ohhh . . .

CHUCK II AND ANNIE: *Puck!*

ANNIE: *Nyugh!*

ALMA: *Pork!* [*Raspberry.*]

CHUCK III: It's "*puck.*"

ALMA: Oh. Sorry.

CHUCKS I, II, III, AMY, ANNIE (*operatic, Wagnerian*): PUCK!

CHUCK: *Ouch.*

CHUCK II: *Oof.*

ANNIE: *Nyugh.*

AMY: Yes.

CHUCK AND CHUCK II: Bingo!

ANNIE: Aaaaaaaaaaand . . .

AMY: Aaaaaaaaaaaaand . . .

CHUCK: Aaaaaaaaaaaaaaaand . . .

CHUCK II: Aaaaaaaaaaaaaaaaaaand . . .

ALMA: (*Raspberry.*)

CHUCK AND CHUCK II, AMY, ANNIE (*Wagnerian*): PUCK!

CHUCK II: *Ouch.*

CHUCK: *Oof.*

ANNIE: Yes!

AMY: Ohhhhhhh . . . ! (*Crescendo to very loud.*)

CHUCK II: Aaaaaaaand . . .

CHUCK: Aaaaaaaaaaand . . .

AMY: Mmmmmmmmmmmmmmm . . .

ANNIE: Mmmmmmmmmmmmmmmmmm . . .

CHUCK AND CHUCK II: AAAAAAAAAAAAAAAAAAAA
AND—

AMY AND ANNIE: MMMMMMMMMMMMMMMMMMM
MMMMMMMMM—

CHUCK III (*quietly*): Bingo.

CHUCK AND CHUCK II, AMY, ANNIE, ALMA: YES!

CHUCK: Okay, so where do we come out?

CHUCK II: What's the score?

CHUCK III (*exhausted*): Are we done yet?

ANNIE: Sorry, Chuck.

AMY: You win. (*Falls into* CHUCK'*s arms.*)

ANNIE: You lose. (*Shows* CHUCK II *the scorecard.*)

CHUCK III: Don't tell me. I lost.

ALMA: You didn't lose. We got nine more holes.

CHUCK III: The nine circles of hell.

ALMA: Well listen. You wanna fuck?

CHUCK III: I resign.

BLACKOUT

SEVEN MENUS

*This play is for
Steve Kaplan*

Seven Menus was first presented by the Manhattan Punch Line Theatre (Steve Kaplan, artistic director) in New York City in January 1989. It was directed by Fred Sanders; the set design was by James Wolk; costume design was by Fontilla Boone; lighting design was by Danianne Mizzy. The cast was as follows:

PAUL	Peter Basch
HAZEL	Melissa Weil
RUTH	Tessie Hogan
JACK	Michael Piontek
BARRY	Gary Cookson
DAWN	Debra Stricklin
PHYLLIS	Nancy McDonald
FLUFF	David Konig

Scene One

A restaurant booth. JACK, RUTH, HAZEL, *and* PAUL. *All in their early thirties. Reading menus.*

PAUL: So why do they call this place Seven Menus?

HAZEL: I really like this place, Ruth.

RUTH: I thought you would.

PAUL: There's only one menu.

HAZEL: "Interesting" decor.

RUTH: Jack introduced me.

JACK: I like to think of this as a higher order of coffee shop. A sort of a transcendental diner.

HAZEL: Well it's the first menu I've ever seen that says Substitutions *Welcomed.*

PAUL: Shouldn't we ask for the other six?

HAZEL: The other six what.

PAUL: The other six menus.

JACK: Paul.

PAUL: Huh?

JACK AND RUTH: *What happened? (This is an old bit between these two, as if to say, "Paul—wake up.")*

PAUL: I knew they were going to say that.

JACK: What happened, Paul?

PAUL: I knew you two were going to say that.

JACK: We always know exactly what we're going to say.

RUTH: That's the great part.

JACK: It is?

RUTH: Well it's *part* of the great part.

JACK: The other part we'll save for later. (*They kiss.*)

HAZEL: Cool it, lovebirds. We've got health regulations to watch out for here.

PAUL: I don't get it.

HAZEL: Are you still searching for the lost menu?

PAUL: Yeah. Why Seven Menus if there's only one?

HAZEL: Maybe it's a translation.

PAUL: Whatever happened to truth in advertising?

HAZEL: Maybe "seven menus" is Chinese for happiness or something.

PAUL: But the place isn't Chinese. I can't tell *what* it is.

JACK: That's what they'll say about you someday, you know.

RUTH: About me?

JACK: You're in advertising, aren't you?

RUTH: I am indeed.

JACK: They'll say whatever happened to Ruth in advertising?

HAZEL: Ouch. Ouch.

JACK: Sorry.

PAUL: Who owns this place, anyway?

JACK: Greeks.

JACK AND RUTH: Of course.

RUTH: Greeks own all restaurants everywhere.

JACK: After inventing tragedy, all that was left was food services.

PAUL: This is all going too fast for me.

HAZEL: Well who wants what. Let's order.

RUTH: Will you look at that menu?

HAZEL: Cajun kielbasa? Char Soo with beansprouts . . . ?

JACK: And Billie Holiday on the jukebox.

PAUL: What's *"joyau de la chasse"*?

JACK: You got me.

HAZEL: "Joy of the chase"?

RUTH: Crown of the chase. Wild fowl stuffed with venison.

JACK: How did you know that?

RUTH: I don't know. Doesn't everybody know that?

JACK: *I* didn't know that.

HAZEL: She must've had it with some other guy, Jack.

JACK: I guess so.

HAZEL: Well I want a salad.

RUTH: Pastrami on rye for me.

JACK (*nibbling one of* RUTH*'s fingers*): I want just this one digit.

RUTH: Finger food, huh.

PAUL: You know what I've got a taste for? French toast.

HAZEL: For *supper*?

PAUL: Actually it's the syrup. What I really want is some sugar.

HAZEL: Well it's a change, anyway.

PAUL: Only there's no French toast on the menu.

JACK: So order another menu.

PAUL: Where *are* the other menus?

HAZEL: Do you know that all the time we were dating, no matter what time of day it was, all Paul would ever order was meatloaf with gravy, mashed potatoes and peas? Every date we ever went out on, morning, noon or night.

PAUL: Or maybe some pancakes . . .

JACK: So Paul used to be a real meatloaf-and-potatoes kinda guy.

RUTH: Now all he wants is sugar.

JACK: It's a sad change.

RUTH: *I* saw it coming.

HAZEL: Anyway, he'd mix the peas in with the mashed potatoes, then swirl in the gravy and sort of beat the meatloaf into submission, then stir the whole mess around on his plate till it was practically soup. And then he'd use a *tablespoon* to eat this goo.

JACK: Does his therapist know about this?

RUTH: I can't believe you married a guy who did things like that, Hazel.

JACK: Sick, baby.

PAUL: What about waffles? Do you think they have waffles at this place?

JACK: They have everything at this place.

PAUL: Everything but what I want.

RUTH: When do you guys leave for the Cape?

PAUL: Saturday morning, ten sharp.

RUTH: Well! *That* sure raised you out of your usual lethargy.

PAUL: You guys should come up and see the house.

JACK: I'd be outclassed.

PAUL: You can test the undertow.

HAZEL: You know, Ruth, I saw Scott when I was up in Providence.

RUTH: Oh yeah? How was that?

JACK: Should I leave the table?

HAZEL: Sit down.

RUTH: Did you talk to him?

HAZEL: Are you kidding? I gave him hell.

RUTH: No.

HAZEL: Not really.

JACK: I think I *will* leave the table.

RUTH: Oh sit down, Tristan.

HAZEL: I said that Ruth had hooked up with this terrific guy named Jack. . . . (JACK *whistles, to drown out her words*.) . . . and that she was very happy . . .

JACK: This is excruciating.

HAZEL: . . . and that he—i.e., Scott—was past past past. Imperfect.

JACK: Did you say a terrific but penniless guy named Jack?

HAZEL: No, I just said terrific.

RUTH: It's all right, darling, I'll pay your check.

HAZEL: I don't know why you should find this excruciating.

JACK: Because I could be him someday. People sitting around and calling me a jerk, and me without the girl.

HAZEL: He *was* a jerk.

JACK: Just reminds you, a little, of the transience of love.

RUTH: Love? Transient?

JACK: You know what I studied in college, don't you?

HAZEL: I'm afraid to ask.

JACK: Romance Languishes.

HAZEL: *Oof.*

PAUL: That's pretty funny.

RUTH: So what did he say? When you talked to him.

HAZEL: Nothing. Just *looked* at me. You know.

RUTH: I can just see it.

JACK: Now I *am* leaving the table.

HAZEL: Oh sit down. We're all adults here.

JACK AND RUTH: We are?

HAZEL: Yeah. Believe it or not, kids, this is adult life.

JACK: Everybody else has three bank accounts and a house in the country.

RUTH: *I* don't have a house in the country.

JACK: But you *will* have a house in the country.

RUTH: Money isn't everything, you know.

JACK: It isn't?

RUTH: No it's not.

JACK: Thank God! (*They kiss.*)

PAUL: Does anybody else want waffles?

HAZEL (*sighs*): True love. Isn't it wonderful?

(*A bell rings. They freeze as they are for a moment.* JACK *exits and* BARRY *enters and takes his place next to* RUTH. *Another bell rings.*)

SCENE TWO

PAUL: But how's the big deal going, Barry?

BARRY: It's going great.

PAUL: Really?

BARRY: We close on it the end of this week.

PAUL: Terrific.

HAZEL: Did you get the price you wanted?

BARRY: *Better* than we wanted.

HAZEL: Sure must be wonderful being with somebody who deals in zillions all day.

BARRY: Parts of zillions, anyway.

HAZEL: A part of a zillion goes a long way.

RUTH: Hang out with somebody in high finance for a while, Hazel. That'll teach you how little you know about the world.

BARRY: So how come they call this place Seven Menus? There's only one menu here.

PAUL: It's part of the place's mystique.

RUTH: Hegel wrestled with that question for years.

HAZEL: So did Kierkegaard.

BARRY: Hegel what?

PAUL: Hasn't Ruth brought you in here before, Barry?

BARRY: No, but I've heard so much about the place I feel like a regular.

HAZEL: We've been coming in here with Ruth and—uh, with Ruth for a long time.

BARRY: Well I'm sure hungry.

PAUL: I'm starving.

RUTH: Who's going to have what?

PAUL: I want something with some sugar.

HAZEL: I feel like having something different. . . .

BARRY: What's good on this menu?

HAZEL: The other six menus.

BARRY: So what do I do with *this* menu?

HAZEL, PAUL, AND RUTH: Order another menu.

BARRY: What?

PAUL: Order another menu when the waiter comes. I went through this once myself, Barry.

RUTH: It's an ancient routine.

(BARRY *suddenly starts to laugh.*)

BARRY: Do you know we had a guy come in this past week with a suitcase full of money?

PAUL: Into your office?

BARRY: Yeah, just walked into the office with a suitcase full of dough. Fifties and hundreds, just laying there loose. Marches in, opens the case, shows them to the receptionist.

HAZEL: Did she offer marriage?

BARRY: No, she called me out there.

HAZEL: Did *you* offer marriage?

RUTH: No, listen to this. It's incredible.

BARRY: So he shows me all this money. There must've been fifty–sixty thousand dollars in this briefcase.

PAUL: I thought it was a suitcase.

BARRY: No, it was a leather briefcase.

PAUL: I thought you said suitcase.

HAZEL: There's a lot of difference between a suitcase and a briefcase full of money.

RUTH: Several years in prison, I think.

BARRY: Anyway, he wanted us to do something with all this money. Comes in off the street and just asks us to *do* something with all this money. He didn't even know what! (*He laughs.*)

HAZEL: So what did you do?

BARRY: Are you kidding? Kicked his ass back out in the street!

HAZEL: Seems a peculiar thing to do to a person with a briefcase full of money.

BARRY: Who knows where he got all that dough. Could've been drugs, embezzlement, who knows.

HAZEL: I figure if somebody walks in with a suitcase or even a briefcase full of happiness, just grab it and run.

BARRY: No such luck, Hazel. Money is never just money.

RUTH: But isn't that incredible?

HAZEL: Yeah . . .

PAUL: That settles it.

RUTH: What.

PAUL: A hot fudge sundae.

HAZEL: I'm glad you're still concentrating on the essentials.

BARRY: Guess it's that time, huh. Think I'll try the meatloaf.

RUTH AND HAZEL: *Uh-oh!*

HAZEL: Meatloaf alert!

BARRY: What's so funny? What's everybody laughing about?

RUTH: Nothing. Just don't mix the meatloaf in with the vegetables.

BARRY: Why not?

HAZEL: Look what happened to us.

PAUL: Private joke, Bare.

RUTH: Paul used to use meatloaf as a sort of mating dance before they got married.

BARRY: Oh.

RUTH: So there's your warning, Hun.

BARRY: Maybe I better go for breast of chicken and play it safe.

HAZEL: Well *I'm* going to try the Welsh rarebit.

PAUL: Hot fudge for me.

RUTH: I'm going to go the whole hog and do the turkey dinner.

BARRY: Actually, speaking of such things . . .

RUTH: Turkeys?

BARRY: Mating dances.

HAZEL: What.

BARRY (*to* RUTH): Should we tell them?

RUTH: You mean now?

BARRY: Why not.

HAZEL: Wake up, Paul.

PAUL: What's going on?

HAZEL: I think something's on the way.

RUTH (*to* BARRY): You or me?

BARRY: Ruth and I are going to get married.

HAZEL: Hooray!

PAUL: Hey, that's terrific, you guys.

HAZEL: Gimme kiss. (*She and* RUTH *kiss.*)

PAUL: Congratulations, that's really terrific.

BARRY: Thank you. Thank you. Thank you.

HAZEL: I've seen this coming for minutes. *Months.*

PAUL: When's the date?

RUTH: We don't know yet.

BARRY: I say the sooner the better.

RUTH: That's so it doesn't interfere with all these deals.

HAZEL: Oh hell, it's just a *marriage.* Run down the road and shanghai the first J.P. you can find.

RUTH: My mother is hysterical.

RUTH AND HAZEL (*together*): Of *course.*

HAZEL: Well I say here's to it. Raise your water glasses, everybody.

BARRY: My glass is dirty.

HAZEL: Raise it anyway. To marriage, and all the rest of it.

ALL: To marriage!

(*Bell. They freeze as they are for a moment.* HAZEL *exits, and* DAWN, *twenty-four, enters and takes her place next to* PAUL. RUTH *takes out a book and reads. Another bell.*)

SCENE THREE

PAUL: Anyway I was thinking that after the wedding Dawn and I could do a week at the Cape, then a week just driving around, then maybe take a couple of weeks in Florida with her parents and get in some scuba diving.

BARRY: You've really shaken Paul out of his usual lethargy, Dawn. He's a totally new man.

DAWN: I guess I'm just an activity-oriented person by nature.

BARRY: He used to be practically comatose till you came along. Paul—*what happened*, huh? What happened?

DAWN: But you know what all that lethargy was.

BARRY: What was that.

DAWN: It was all that sugar! That's why Paul's always been so low-energy. It was a sugar O.D.

PAUL: Now I'm off sugar I'm a dynamo.

BARRY: You sure look trim.

PAUL: Do I look trim?

RUTH: I didn't know you could scuba dive, Paul.

PAUL: Huh?

RUTH: I said I didn't know that you could scuba dive.

PAUL: Dawn's going to teach me.

DAWN: I love scuba diving. I've been doing it since, God, since I was about *ten*.

RUTH: So you're still using the house on the Cape?

PAUL: What, me?

RUTH: Yeah. I thought . . .

PAUL: No, Hazel and I split it up. Half a month each.

BARRY: That's a fair arrangement.

PAUL: Yeah, it all works out okay.

BARRY: That's very equitable.

DAWN: It's the least she could do, you know.

RUTH: I beg pardon?

DAWN: Hazel. I mean she and Paul bought the house together, fifty-fifty. And you don't want 'em to just sell it, right?

RUTH: Mm.

PAUL: Anyway, you two guys'll have to come up for a weekend.

BARRY: There's an idea.

DAWN: Yeah, come up and test the water.

PAUL: Get a change of air.

BARRY: Or you two could come up to our place.

DAWN: Do you have a house too?

PAUL: They've got a *real* country house.

BARRY: Up in the mountains.

DAWN: Oh I *love* the mountains.

BARRY: Southern Vermont.

DAWN: I *love* Vermont.

BARRY: Do you like to ski?

RUTH: She *loves* to ski.

DAWN: I *do* love to ski.

BARRY (*to* RUTH): Hey.

RUTH: What. Something wrong?

DAWN: What's the matter?

BARRY: Nothing.

RUTH: Must've been something I ate. Not enough sugar or something.

BARRY: Maybe if you put the goddamn book down. . . .

PAUL: You know what I'm going to have?

DAWN: You don't even have to tell me.

PAUL: Meatloaf and potatoes and gravy.

DAWN: I knew it!

PAUL: With peas.

DAWN: I knew it! Every time we go out, night or day, it's always meatloaf and mashed potatoes and peas.

RUTH: And then he mashes them all together on his plate? Mixes the peas into the potatoes and stirs it all around?

DAWN: How did you know?

RUTH: Womanly intuition. But maybe you'll get a *quarter* of the house on the Cape. Someday.

DAWN: What's she talking about?

PAUL: Just a private joke.

DAWN: A quarter of the house . . . ?

BARRY: What do you do for a living, Dawn?

DAWN: I'm a food therapist.

RUTH: A *food therapist*?

DAWN: Uh-huh. So I treat things like obesity, and anorexia, and—you know—things like that.

BARRY: Sounds fascinating.

DAWN: I think it's a terrific way of finding out what makes people tick.

RUTH: Or burp, I suppose.

PAUL: You should hear some of her stories. Like this guy who was so fat he had to have his bed reinforced so he didn't just disappear right through the floor.

DAWN: That was due to a gland condition, though.

PAUL: Guy could've ended up in China!

DAWN: There was nothing the man could do about it since it was all glandular.

BARRY: Incredible.

DAWN: Everything is glands when you get right down to it.

RUTH: Are we about ready to order?

DAWN: Then there's bulimia.

RUTH: Could we save bulimia for after dessert?

PAUL: Sure. Sure.

BARRY: Well who wants what.

DAWN: I haven't even had time to study this menu.

PAUL: Meatloaf for me.

DAWN: They have *pheasant* here?

PAUL: They have everything here.

RUTH: Here's something. (*Refers to her book.*) New statistics. Single women live longer than married women.

DAWN: Wow.

PAUL: Really?

DAWN: So single women live longer than married women?

RUTH: I think I just said that. But listen to *this* (*she is about to read more from her book*)—

BARRY (*interrupting*): Oh come on.

RUTH: Come on what.

BARRY: You ought to be able to see through that.

RUTH: See through what.

BARRY: You're in advertising, you know how to juggle figures. You can crunch a bunch of numbers any way you want.

DAWN: What else does it say?

RUTH: It says that single women are also overwhelmingly happier than married women.

DAWN: I didn't know that.

BARRY: Happy according to who?

RUTH: Happy according to themselves.

BARRY: Here's a woman hauling down a huge salary who can't see through a lot of crooked figures.

RUTH: Are we going to order? If we're not, I've got things to do at home.

BARRY: Just hold your horses, okay? Hold your horses. We'll order.

DAWN: You know, I was sitting on the bus the other day reading this book of stories, and I was laughing out loud—

PAUL: That book you read to me from?

DAWN: Yeah, and I was laughing really hard, and there was this guy sitting next to me, kind of an old guy, and he says, "Whatcha reading," and I said, "Stories."

BARRY: He was probably trying to pick you up.

DAWN: But listen to this. He says, "Looks like those stories are pretty funny," and I said some of them were funny, and *then* he says: "Have you got any heartrending ones in there?"

BARRY: Huh.

DAWN: Isn't that funny?

PAUL: "Have you got any heartrending ones in there . . . "

DAWN: I thought it was kind of sad.

BARRY: Yeah.

PAUL: How's business with you, Barry?

BARRY: Oh, you know. Nothing ever changes.

(*Bell.* RUTH *and* PAUL *leave.* DAWN *joins* BARRY *on his side of the table, and he puts an arm around her.* PHYLLIS *sits at the table.* FLUFF *stands behind her. Bell.*)

SCENE FOUR

BARRY: But once in a while you want something different.

DAWN: We sure don't do this all the time, you know.

BARRY: You want to try something new.

DAWN: In fact we've never done it before in all our lives.

BARRY: New faces, new bodies, new sensations.

DAWN: I never even *read* those swinger magazines.

BARRY: Makes for a little sauce, you know what I mean?

DAWN: I mean, isn't it a little strange, advertising yourself for sex?

BARRY (*referring to* FLUFF): Does your, uh, friend want to sit and join the party, or . . . ?

PHYLLIS: You two don't have any serious social diseases, do you?

DAWN AND BARRY (*together*): Social dis—? What, social diseases?

DAWN: Oh no. No. I've never had a single thing like that.

BARRY: I had the clap a couple of times in college, but who didn't?

FLUFF: Do you have a very large penis?

BARRY: Excuse me?

FLUFF: Your penis. I have to watch out for my friend here.

DAWN: But here we are talking about penises and we don't even know your names!

FLUFF: I'm Simon.

PHYLLIS: No he's not.

FLUFF: I'm Charlie.

PHYLLIS: No he's not.

FLUFF: I am the Catch of the Day.

PHYLLIS: I'm Phyllis and he's Fluff.

BARRY: "Fluff"—?

FLUFF (*holds up four fingers*): Yeah. Three *f*'s.

BARRY: Kind of an interesting name.

FLUFF: Anglo-Saxon.

DAWN (*to* PHYLLIS): Is he part of our—you know—liaison?

PHYLLIS: He's along for the ride.

BARRY: So are you guys gonna eat . . . or shall we retire for some fun?

PHYLLIS: You're going to have to do a lot better than that. (*Picks up the menu.*) Seven Menus, huh . . .

BARRY: Yeah, you noticed the name? It's part of the place's mystique. Hegel once wrote a book about why they call this place Seven Menus.

FLUFF: There's no mystery about the name.

BARRY: I beg pardon?

FLUFF: You get a different menu depending on when you come in here.

BARRY: But I've been in here all hours of the day and it's always the same menu.

FLUFF: Sure. But *you're* different.

BARRY: Huh?

FLUFF: You're not the same person at supper that you were at breakfast. Breakfast, brunch, lunch, afternoon snack, cocktails, supper and midnight munch. These are the Seven Ages of Man. (*Pause.*)

DAWN: Didn't your ad say that you're in advertising?

PHYLLIS: Yeah, I run an ad agency.

DAWN: That must be great!

PHYLLIS: It has its moments. How's the pastitsio?

BARRY: It's good, it's good. I never tried it, but everything is good here.

DAWN: I always kind of wished I went into advertising when I had the chance.

BARRY: Do we need to talk about advertising? Let's talk about your-place-or-ours.

DAWN: Barry's ex used to be in advertising.

PHYLLIS: Really.

DAWN: God she was a terrible person.

BARRY: Yeah well . . .

FLUFF: I always liked her, actually.

DAWN: Barry's ex?

FLUFF: Yeah. I thought she was terrific.

DAWN: Did you know her?

FLUFF: Warm. Funny. Vulnerable. Lemon-flavored. Static-free. I still miss the bitch, to tell you the truth.

DAWN: What *are* you? I mean—what do you do for a living?

FLUFF: I don't do anything. I live off of her.

BARRY: Nice work if you can get it.

PHYLLIS: But he also knows the true meaning of tenderness.

BARRY: I'm in the middle of a career change, myself.

DAWN: He got fired.

BARRY: I used to be in high finance, but lately I've been thinking I might go into food services.

FLUFF: *Food services* . . .

BARRY: Yeah.

DAWN: Anyway, how did you—

BARRY: Food services is a very, very, very interesting field.

DAWN: But how did you get to run a whole agency?

BARRY: Dawn here is in food therapy. I was thinking she and I could team up. I could cater the food, and she could provide the therapy, after.

FLUFF: Brilliant.

BARRY: Just stay away from high finance, that's my advice.

DAWN: Oh Barry . . .

BARRY: You get into some weird deals and you are gone, buddy.

DAWN: Are we gonna order now?

BARRY: You know one time a guy came into our office with a couple of hundred thousand dollars in a suitcase?

DAWN: Oh come on, Bare.

BARRY: What, come on.

DAWN: Not that story.

BARRY: What story.

DAWN: He tells this story all the time. About this guy who brought in some money in a briefcase.

BARRY: A suitcase.

DAWN: Okay, a suitcase.

FLUFF: So what happened?

BARRY: Nothing happened. It's not important.

FLUFF: No really. What happened?

BARRY: Nothing happened. We kicked the guy out. End of story.

(*Bell.* BARRY *and* FLUFF *exit.* JACK *enters and sits next to* PHYLLIS. *Bell.*)

SCENE FIVE

DAWN: But that's not the end of the story. Because I marched in there, and I put my hands on his desk and I said, *"Advertising is about making choices."*

PHYLLIS: Ten points.

DAWN: Was I not a food therapist? Did I not design diets for people? And what are diets all about?

PHYLLIS: Making the right choices.

DAWN: So who's the best person for this account?

PHYLLIS: You are.

DAWN: And he gave it to me right on the spot. A million-dollar account!

PHYLLIS: And she lived happily ever after.

DAWN: You never should've left the agency, Phil.

PHYLLIS: Ohhh no . . .

DAWN: Just think what you could be doing now.

PHYLLIS: I'm very happy as a housewife, thank you.

DAWN: Nobody's happy as a housewife.

PHYLLIS: I have found my counterrevolutionary niche—roasting meat on a spit for a man who always comes home.

DAWN: I thought that I'd found *my* niche, and God was I wrong! Do you know I ran into one of my old patients in the street the other day and I couldn't even remember his name? God I was so embarrassed. Sometimes I wonder how I could stand spending eight and ten hours a day with those people.

PHYLLIS: I ran into an old boyfriend last week and I couldn't remember his name.

DAWN: You're kidding. A client I can believe, but a *boyfriend*?

PHYLLIS: Well—life is long, men short. In all too many cases. (*She and* DAWN *laugh.*) Not *all* men, though. (*Nudges* JACK.)

I'm talking about you, Jack.

JACK: Oh. Sorry.

DAWN: What she was saying was, she had found her perfect niche with you.

JACK: Yeah well. If you've got a niche, scratch it. Sorry.

DAWN: What?

JACK: Nothing.

PHYLLIS: Just Jack being funny.

DAWN: But what about *your* big deal?

JACK: The what?

DAWN: The deal out West. Did you close on it?

JACK: Oh. Yeah, we closed on it.

DAWN: So now you can pay off the house on the Vineyard and you'll be set for life.

JACK: I guess.

PHYLLIS: Are you okay?

DAWN: Jack . . .

JACK: Huh?

DAWN: *What happened?* You know?

JACK: What did you say . . . ?

DAWN: Oh nothing. Just something stupid *Barry* picked up from his ex.

PHYLLIS: You mean his *ex*-ex.

DAWN: Ruth. The dragon lady.

PHYLLIS: I saw Barry the other day.

DAWN: Oh yeah? What did he have to say for himself?

PHYLLIS: Not much.

DAWN: I'll bet. Does he have a job yet?

PHYLLIS: I don't think so. He asked me how you were.

DAWN: I hope you gave him hell.

PHYLLIS: I said that you were fine.

DAWN: Jerk . . . (JACK *suddenly shifts as if he's about to rise.*)

PHYLLIS: Jack, what's the matter?

JACK: Nothing. Nothing. Just—nothing.

PHYLLIS: Do you want to go home?

JACK: No. Let's stay. Let's order something.

PHYLLIS: Are you sure?

JACK: Yeah. Let's chow down. Or chow up. Or chow in some direction. . . .

PHYLLIS: You don't have a headache, do you?

JACK: Nope. Nope nope nope nope . . .

PHYLLIS: Scratch my neck. (*He lightly scratches the nape of her neck.*)

DAWN: Anybody know what *"joyau de la chasse"* is? I always forget to ask.

PHYLLIS: Joy of the chase?

JACK: Crown of the chase. Wild fowl stuffed with venison.

PHYLLIS: How did you know that?

JACK: I don't know. Doesn't everybody know that?

PHYLLIS: *I* didn't know that.

DAWN: I guess he must've had it with some other woman, Phil.

PHYLLIS: I guess so.

DAWN: That is a great wife you got there, you know.

JACK: I know.

DAWN: Don't you ever lose her, mister.

JACK: I wasn't planning on it.

DAWN: That girl is solid gold.

PHYLLIS: Maybe I'd better leave.

DAWN: Oh sit down. We're all adults here.

JACK: We are?

(*Bell.* JACK *exits. Another bell.*)

SCENE SIX

DAWN: I saw Jack today.

PHYLLIS: Oh yeah . . . ? How's he?

DAWN: Maybe you should give him a call.

PHYLLIS: I think I'm past Jack, thank you. Past Jack, past Bob, past Allen, past Manuel, past Fred, past Igor . . .

DAWN: But are you past waiters? That one over there is kinda cute.

PHYLLIS: Oh come on.

DAWN: We could order up a little meatloaf.

PHYLLIS: I'm also past picking up strange waiters in restaurants.

DAWN: I don't know. He doesn't look so strange to me.

PHYLLIS: Don't you ever give up?

DAWN: Nope.

PHYLLIS: You know—I don't honestly know what I'd do without you.

(*Bell.* DAWN *leaves. Bell.*)

SCENE SEVEN

PHYLLIS: Waiter! (*She smiles at him sweetly.*)

BLACKOUT

MERE MORTALS

*This play is in memory
of my father*

Mere Mortals was first presented at Ensemble Studio Theatre in New York City in June 1990. It was directed by Jason McConnell Buzas; the set design was by Linda Giering Balmuth; costume design by Leslie McGovern; lighting design by Greg MacPherson. The cast was as follows:

JOE Robert Pastorelli
CHARLIE Brian Smiar
FRANK Anthony LaPaglia

A girder on the fiftieth floor of a new, unfinished skyscraper. One end of the girder is still unattached and hanging in open space. JOE *is sitting astride the girder, near its attached end. He is unwrapping a sandwich and reading a newspaper with intense absorption. A bird sails by.* JOE *doesn't notice. A couple of small clouds sail by.* JOE *doesn't notice.*

JOE (*something in the paper*): Unbelievable.

(*We hear* CHARLIE *singing. A moment later, he and* FRANK *enter, with lunch pails.* FRANK *is thirty-five,* CHARLIE *sixty.* CHARLIE *stops to belt the end of his song.*)

CHARLIE (*singing*): "I'm the man! I'm the man I'm the man I'm the man! I'm the man who broke the bank at Monte Carlo!" (*He heads onward.*) Hey Joe.

JOE: Hey Charlie.

FRANK: Hey Joe.

JOE: Hey Frank. (CHARLIE *goes out to the very end of the girder.* FRANK *sits midway out and opens his lunch pail.*)

CHARLIE: Think we're gonna make fifty today?

FRANK: Looks like it.

CHARLIE: Fifty stories down, fifty stories to go. I think we're gonna have this baby all punched in a week ahead of schedule.

JOE: Yeah . . .

CHARLIE: And what a view to lunch by, huh?

FRANK: Beautiful.

CHARLIE: Jersey.

FRANK: Yeah.

CHARLIE: *My home.*

FRANK: This is what I love about working up here. We eat like kings.

CHARLIE: So. What's the bill of fare today? Frankie, what've you got?

FRANK (*peering into his sandwich*): I think it's liverwurst.

CHARLIE: Joe? Howbout you?

JOE (*reading*): Pickle and pimento loaf.

FRANK: Wait a minute. It's not liverwurst. It's tuna. I think.

CHARLIE: Well *I* got corned beef and pastrami.

FRANK: Charlie, is that tuna, or liverwurst? (*Realizing.*) You got corned *beef*?

CHARLIE: And Poupon mustard.

FRANK: On a normal Tuesday? What's the occasion?

CHARLIE: Who says there's an occasion?

FRANK: You hear that, Joe? Charlie's got corned beef and pastrami on a normal Tuesday.

CHARLIE: On bakery pumpernickel.

FRANK: On bakery pumpernickel. With Poupon mustard.

JOE (*not interested*): Very nice. (*A small cloud passes by.*)

CHARLIE: Look at all those poor souls down there, have to eat their lunch at sea level. (*Sings.*) "I'm the man who broke the bank at Monte Carlo!"

FRANK: What's the news today, Joe? Something hot in the paper?

JOE (*doesn't look up*): Hm?

FRANK: Some kinda . . . you know . . .

CHARLIE: International developments?

FRANK: International developments? How's things in Europe? Any news?

JOE: The news is that history is a cesspool.

FRANK: Oh.

JOE: As it always was. We also find out that a woman in Astoria Queens lived with a guy for *fifteen years,* didn't know the guy had five other wives.

FRANK: Five other wives?

JOE: In the same *neighborhood.*

FRANK: Did you hear this, Charlie?

CHARLIE: Many things are possible in this world.

FRANK: A guy with that many wives—is that still bigamy?

JOE: It's geometry.

FRANK: Huh. Well gimme the TV page, will you? Let's see what's on the tube.

CHARLIE: Don't let me hear anything about TV.

FRANK: I just want to see—

CHARLIE: Don't let me hear no talk about TV. We got bowling tonight.

FRANK: I just want to see what I'm missing.

CHARLIE: Speaking of which, who's in for tonight?

FRANK: I'm in.

CHARLIE: Joe, are you in?

JOE: I can't this week, Charlie.

CHARLIE: You want to bowl a few games tonight?

JOE: I got things I got to do at home.

CHARLIE: What, you gotta nail up some doilies in your wife's powder room or something?

JOE: I got some things I got to do at—

CHARLIE: So do 'em tomorrow.

JOE: Bridget wants me to do 'em tonight.

CHARLIE: So bring her along and do 'em tomorrow.

JOE: I can't do 'em tomorrow, I—

CHARLIE: Hey who's the king in your house, anyway? Who is the king? Who makes the rules?

FRANK: Gentlemen . . .

JOE: When Maggie wanted you to put in that new floor, you didn't bowl for two weeks, Charlie.

CHARLIE: That was different.

JOE: And because you couldn't bowl, you wouldn't let *us* bowl either.

CHARLIE: That was different.

JOE: Yeah why was it so different?

CHARLIE: Just don't get small on me, Joe, okay?

JOE: Why was it so—

CHARLIE: I hate it when you get *small* on me like that.

FRANK: Gentlemen, *please!* (*After a moment.*)

JOE: And it's not doilies.

FRANK: Joe. (JOE *is quiet.*)

CHARLIE: How's your wife doin', Frankie?

FRANK: She's good.

CHARLIE: The doctor fix her all up and everything?

FRANK: Looks like it. She was out there mowing the grass yesterday.

CHARLIE: That's a sign.

FRANK: That's a sign. But howbout that lawn mower you just bought, Charlie? How's that working?

CHARLIE: Aaaaah, it's busted.

FRANK: No.

CHARLIE: Yeah, it's . . .

FRANK: Already?

CHARLIE: Yeah.

FRANK: So did you take it back?

CHARLIE: I don't know why I ever cut my grass in the first place. I *like* it long. I like to sit on my porch and look at it long. Where do you think the word "lawn" comes from in the first place? From "long," because grass was always *long*. Originally people said, "I'm gonna plant some seeds and grow a long." Then some moron thought he'd be different and cut his long short. The rest is the history of fashion.

FRANK: I didn't know that. (JOE *snickers*.)

CHARLIE: You say something, Joe?

JOE: Who, me? No, I didn't say anything. (*A paper floats by.* CHARLIE *plucks it out of the air, glances at it, and lets it float away again*.)

FRANK (*looks up and calls*): Yo, Peptak! You got any of those sugar cubes? (*He holds out the cup of his thermos and a sugar cube drops into it from above*.) Thanks! (*An air mattress floats by. No comment from any of them*.)

CHARLIE: You guys ever think about hang-gliding home from here?

FRANK: Hang-gliding home?

CHARLIE: Yeah, instead of driving or taking the Path?

FRANK: Wouldn't you have to learn how to hang-glide first?

CHARLIE: Well sure, you'd learn. But then after you wrapped up work you could just strap on your wings—walk off the top floor—and sail home. Be the first person in history to fly from Thirty-second Street and Tenth Avenue to Tenafly, New Jersey. With a fabulous view all the way. (*Small pause.*) Maybe after I retire.

FRANK: You know I been sitting here eating this thing and I still don't know if it's tuna or liverwurst?

CHARLIE: Yeah well that's all the ozone up here.

FRANK: The what?

CHARLIE: The carbon dioxide at this altitude compresses the things in your nose, and you can't taste nothing. (JOE *snickers, louder than before.*)

CHARLIE: Did you say something, Joe?

JOE: Not me. I guess the carbon dioxide was compressing my nose or something.

FRANK (*from the newspaper*): Speaking of flying, Charlie, they got that movie about the Lindbergh kid on again tonight.

CHARLIE: They got the what?

FRANK: That show about the Lindbergh baby who got kidnapped, with—

CHARLIE: Let me see that. (*He grabs the paper.*)

FRANK: Hey, what's up? What the hell are you doing?

CHARLIE: I just want to see. (*Reads intently.*)

FRANK: Did you see that movie that time it was on?

CHARLIE: Yeah . . .

FRANK: With Anthony Hopkins, as what's his name . . .

CHARLIE: Bruno Hauptmann.

FRANK: Hey didn't that happen someplace around—?

CHARLIE: Hopewell, New Jersey.

JOE: What are they bringing that turkey back for?

CHARLIE: "Turkey"?

JOE: Yeah, who wants to see that garbage all over again?

CHARLIE: It happens to be a very thoughtful movie, for your information. And as it happens today is the anniversary of the day that Charles Lindbergh's baby was kidnapped.

JOE: That happened fifty years ago! What's the big deal about—

CHARLIE: Jesus Christ died on Easter, they show *The King of Kings* that weekend.

FRANK: Gentlemen . . .

CHARLIE: If you'd ever done anything more important than glue your wife's cat pictures into a photo album, they'd show the *Joe Morelli Story* on *your* birthday. Does that explain to you why the movie is on today?

FRANK: Gentlemen, please!

CHARLIE: And don't let me hear the word "turkey."

FRANK: Hey what's with you today, Charlie? What's the matter?

CHARLIE: Nothing's the matter.

FRANK: You're acting all weird.

CHARLIE: I'm not weird.

FRANK: So what's up?

JOE: Turkey.

CHARLIE: I TOLD YOU I DON'T WANT TO HEAR THE WORD "TURKEY"!

FRANK: Something sure seems up.

CHARLIE: Nothing is up. Forget about it. Nothing's up.

FRANK: Here, bird. (*He whistles to a passing bird and tosses it a crumb.* CHARLIE *takes a cupcake out of his lunch pail, unobtrusively puts a candle in, and lights it.*)

FRANK: What the heck is *that?*

CHARLIE: What does it look like? It's a cupcake.

FRANK: Hey Joe, will you look at this?

JOE: Isn't that nice. Maggie made him a cupcake.

CHARLIE: My wife did *not* make me this cupcake, I *bought* this cupcake.

FRANK: What's the . . . you know . . .

CHARLIE: Celebration?

FRANK: The celebration, Charlie?

CHARLIE: Who says there's a celebration?

FRANK: Corned beef and pastrami and a chocolate cupcake?

CHARLIE (*pointing to the cupcake*): If you will notice—a somber color. Maybe I'm observing a very solemn day for some private reason.

JOE: Next thing you know he's going to be putting out doilies around his house.

CHARLIE: That's it, Morelli!

FRANK: Gentlemen—

JOE: And your taste in movies is lousy!

FRANK: Gentlemen—

JOE: And if you ask me, Charles Lindbergh is overrated.

CHARLIE: Overrated?

JOE: Yeah, overrated! So he flew across the—

CHARLIE: The greatest hero in American history?

JOE: He flew across the ocean. *Big deal.*

CHARLIE: Oh big deal, huh?

JOE: Yeah. And as for the Lindbergh baby—who *cares?*

CHARLIE: Who cares?

JOE: Yeah who the hell cares, it's old news!

CHARLIE: Oh yeah?

JOE: It's ancient history that kid got stolen.

CHARLIE: Well for your information—

JOE: Working people get kidnapped every day in the world and they don't make no movies about *them.*

CHARLIE: Maybe they're not as important as the Lindbergh baby.

JOE: So why am I supposed to care about the goddamn Lindbergh baby?

CHARLIE: You don't care about the Lindbergh baby?

JOE: No, I don't care about the Lindbergh baby!

CHARLIE: You don't have any feeling for the Lindbergh baby?

JOE: No I don't have any feeling for the Lindbergh baby!

CHARLIE: Well for your information, *I am the Lindbergh baby!* (*Long pause.*)

FRANK: You're the . . . ?

CHARLIE: *Yes*. I am the Lindbergh baby. I am the rightful son of Charles Lindbergh, kidnapped from the home of my parents, and I didn't mean to tell you but you forced me into it. And the hell if I will listen to my family being insulted! So there!

JOE: You're the——?

CHARLIE: Yes.

FRANK: But your name is Petrossian.

CHARLIE: Oh sure. That's what I was brought up to *think* my name was.

JOE: YOU THINK YOU'RE THE LINDBERGH BABY?

CHARLIE: Go to hell, Joe.

JOE: Have you gone off your head?

CHARLIE: No I have not gone off my head.

JOE: I don't believe this!

CHARLIE: Yeah well the truth is always strange at first sight. So live with it.

JOE: Do you know that there are separate asylums to hold all the people who think they're the Lindbergh baby?

CHARLIE: Just mind your own business, will you? Read your newspaper. Stick to pickle and pimento loaf, Smalltime.

FRANK: Charlie, there *are* people who might wonder a little, if you claimed to be the Lindbergh baby.

CHARLIE: But it all fits, doesn't it? I mean—"Charles"? "Charlie"? Was I not born in New Jersey and brought up in the town of Hopewell, where the crime was perpetrated?

FRANK: He *was* brought up in Hopewell, Joe.

JOE: Yeah? That makes about fifty thousand other Lindbergh babies.

CHARLIE: Well they're impostors.

FRANK: I thought the police found the kid's body.

CHARLIE: That was another kid's body.

FRANK: Whose body?

CHARLIE: I don't know whose body. But it wasn't *my* body.

FRANK: Obviously not. . . . How come you kept this a secret all these years, Charlie?

CHARLIE: Well naturally a lot of people wouldn't believe me.

JOE: OH REALLY?

CHARLIE: Plus I was already pretty well established as Charles Petrossian. You know—driver's license, credit cards, bank account . . .

FRANK: Sure, it's hard to make a change.

CHARLIE: But mostly I didn't want to upset the feelings of my true mother, Anne Morrow Lindbergh.

JOE: Whose books are bullshit.

CHARLIE: You shut your trap about my mother!

FRANK: Come on, Joe, you know better than that.

JOE: Have you read her books?

CHARLIE: Yes I have and I think they're very beautiful.

JOE: She made a goddamn fortune offa you, writing about that kidnapping.

CHARLIE: It happened to be a very traumatic experience for her.

JOE: That don't mean she has to go peddle it on the street corner. You oughtta ask for a cut of her royalties. You could retire early, take up *hang-gliding*.

CHARLIE: I'm through talking to you.

FRANK: Joe's got a good point, Charlie. You ought to contact the family. You could try to pick up your inheritance. You coulda been a rich guy, Charlie!

CHARLIE: Actually . . . I did write to mother, once.

FRANK: You did?

CHARLIE: Yeah. But she never answered back. I figure the letter never got to her.

FRANK: Did you tell her—you know—who you were?

CHARLIE: I *hinted* who I was.

JOE: Oh sure. "Dear Mom. *Guess who?*" And then he signed it, "Your loving son, Charles Petrossian. P.S. Send the inheritance."

CHARLIE: Knock it off.

JOE: Real subtle.

CHARLIE: Anyway I told her how I was from her area. That's how I put it, I said that I was "from her *area.*"

FRANK: That's a hint.

JOE: Sigmund Freud would've had a picnic.

CHARLIE: I told her how I saw their house lots of times.

FRANK: You saw the house you were kidnapped from?

CHARLIE: Sure. I used to go by it all the time when I was a kid. Then later on when I knew who I really was I used to drive out there sometimes and just park and look at it. I'd park under this tree and sit there thinking to myself, This is yours, Charlie. This is your kingdom.

FRANK: So your old man flew the Atlantic in the *Spirit of St. Louis.*

CHARLIE: And my grandfather was ambassador to Mexico.

FRANK: I didn't know that.

CHARLIE: Yeah, my mother's father.

FRANK: I seen the movie lots of times on the late show, *The Spirit of St. Louis*. Must be great, having Jimmy Stewart play your father and all.

CHARLIE: I wrote to Jimmy once, under my nom de plume of Petrossian.

FRANK: He ever answer back?

CHARLIE: I got a signed picture in the mail.

FRANK: You never told me that!

CHARLIE: Yeah.

FRANK: You never told me you had a signed picture of Jimmy Stewart!

CHARLIE: Well I been keeping it a secret in case people start getting ideas about my true identity. Somebody puts a few clues together, it could have repercussions.

JOE: Yeah, they'd throw you in the loony bin.

CHARLIE: Go ahead. Scoff if you will!

FRANK: But this means Anthony Hopkins didn't really do it.

CHARLIE: You mean kidnap me?

FRANK: Yeah.

CHARLIE: Obviously not. Not unless he was in league with the Petrossian family, and handed me over to them.

FRANK: Yeah—what *about* the Petrossians' role in all this?

CHARLIE: My foster parents, as I like to think of them? Pawns in a bigger game, Frank. Pawns in a bigger game.

FRANK: But how did you make the transition? I mean, from being a Lindbergh to being a Petrossian?

CHARLIE: Let me just say, I got my ideas, Frankie.

FRANK: You know it's very funny you should be saying all this.

CHARLIE: What, that I've been the Lindbergh baby all these years and you never knew it?

FRANK: Yeah. Because you see, I'm the son of Czar Nicholas the Second of Russia.

CHARLIE: No.

FRANK: Yeah.

CHARLIE: You're kidding.

FRANK: It's the truth.

CHARLIE: The kid that got killed in the Russian Revolution?

FRANK: That's me. The heir to the throne of Moscow.

CHARLIE: Holy shit.

FRANK: And Sovereign of the Ukraine.

CHARLIE: I saw that movie. *Nicholas and What's-Her-Name*.

FRANK: Alexandra. That was *my* mother.

CHARLIE: But I thought you got shot.

FRANK: A faithful servant smuggled me out. Nobody knows I survived.

CHARLIE: And you had Laurence Olivier in your movie and everything. I mean, Anthony Hopkins is one thing—but Sir Laurence Olivier!

FRANK: Yeah, I felt pretty honored, having him in my movie. Though I did have a few quibbles about the, you know, historical details.

CHARLIE: So what's your real name?

FRANK: Alexei Nikolaievitch Romanoff.

CHARLIE: By what name would you prefer to be called?

FRANK: Why don't you just keep calling me Frank. It'll be easier.

CHARLIE: Besides protecting your incognito.

JOE: THE CZAR OF RUSSIA?

CHARLIE: Now Joe—

JOE: *THE CZAR OF RUSSIA?*

CHARLIE: I don't want to hear a word from you, Joe.

JOE: Do you know how old you'd have to be, to be the Czar of Russia?

CHARLIE: Never you mind, Frank.

JOE: You'd have to be ninety years old!

CHARLIE: You want to hurt his feelings?

JOE: And a hemophiliac!

FRANK: I've always been a heavy bleeder.

JOE: That don't make you the goddamn Czar of Russia! I mean, the Lindbergh baby is one thing, but—

CHARLIE: Will you just shut up? Please? Shut up? You're on a lot of very sensitive ground. We are talking families, Joe. And Frank here lost everybody in the Revolution, so have a little sympathy. You got orphans here.

JOE: Okay then, Alexei. How do you know all this? How do you know you're the head honcho of the Ukraine?

FRANK: Well . . . one day I saw this picture in a book, a picture of Moscow with the . . . you know . . . the Kremlin, and those domes—

CHARLIE: Yeah, those onion-shaped domes.

FRANK: And I said to myself, I've been there! I've been there sometime! It was like I could remember it.

CHARLIE: Of course you'd remember it. Those communist bastards tried to rub you out there.

FRANK: And then when I saw that movie it was like I knew all the streets. Before they'd even go around a corner I'd know what was going to be on the other side. It was home.

CHARLIE: Musta been painful.

FRANK: It was pretty painful.

CHARLIE: Seeing everything you lost out on.

FRANK: It only got really bad when I had to watch myself get killed.

CHARLIE: Understandably, Alexei. Understandably. But how's your Russian these days?

FRANK: Oh, I've forgotten most of it by now.

CHARLIE: The whole trauma probably made you—you know—

FRANK: Repress it.

CHARLIE: Repress it. Plus the strain of having to maintain your daily identity as Frank Mikula. Have you told Phyllis?

FRANK: No, she doesn't know. I'll probably have to tell her sometime, though.

CHARLIE: I think she'll understand.

FRANK: I just have to wait for the right—you know—

CHARLIE: Circumstances.

FRANK: Circumstances.

CHARLIE: She'd probably be pretty surprised to find out she's the queen of Russia.

FRANK: Czarina.

CHARLIE: Huh?

FRANK: The wife of the czar is the czarina.

CHARLIE: Is that proof, Joe? Is that the proof? I say "queen," he says "czarina." He's got the facts at the tips of his fingers.

JOE: I know how cars work, but that don't make me an Oldsmobile.

FRANK: Peace, gentlemen.

CHARLIE: Just think. If we'd 'a had you over there running things all these years, the Berlin Wall woulda gotten taken down a lot sooner than it did—after not being built in the *first* place.

FRANK: Yeah. That's the hardest thing about being—you know—

CHARLIE: Who you are.

FRANK: Who I am. Knowing what I could do for world peace.

CHARLIE: Have you ever contemplated the restoration of your throne?

FRANK: I think I should leave that to the will of the people.

CHARLIE: Well if things had worked out different, I can't think of anybody I'd rather have on the Russian throne than you, Frank.

FRANK: Thanks, Charlie.

CHARLIE: Well I'll be goddamned. To think all this time we never knew it. You didn't know about me, and I didn't know about you. And Joe didn't know about either one of us. . . . (*Silence. They turn and look at* JOE.)

FRANK: So, Joe . . .

JOE: Yeah, what?

FRANK: Who are *you?*

JOE: I'm not anybody.

FRANK: Really, I mean.

JOE: I'm not anybody.

FRANK: *Really.*

JOE: I'm Joe Morelli. Period.

FRANK: I'm not talking about that.

JOE: I'm Superman.

FRANK: I mean really.

JOE: I'm nobody.

FRANK: Underneath it all.

JOE: I'm nobody. I'm just another guy on the street. (*Pause.*) But in a previous lifetime I was Marie Antoinette.

CHARLIE: No shit!

JOE: Yeah, that was me!

FRANK: The let-'em-eat-cake lady?

JOE: I said that in 1793. "Let them eat cake!"

CHARLIE: Isn't that something.

FRANK: I knew you were *some*body.

CHARLIE: Frank gets shot up by the Reds and you have your head chopped off in Paris.

JOE: Yeah. One minute I'm standing on a scaffold in a diamond tiara, the next minute I'm Joe Morelli in Weehawken.

CHARLIE: Must be pretty disconcerting.

JOE: To say the least. But I do remember kneeling down on the thing there, the guillotine, and the blade— (*Construction whistle, off.*)

CHARLIE: Aaah shit.

FRANK: Already?

JOE: It's one o'clock?

CHARLIE: That's what the company says.

JOE: Jesus. (*They pack up their things.*) But listen, you guys—you can't tell anybody.

FRANK: You forget who you're talking to.

JOE: I don't want this getting around.

FRANK: We know that.

JOE: People would think I was kinda weird.

FRANK: We will be as the tomb.

JOE: You swear?

CHARLIE: Of course we swear.

FRANK: We're all in the same—you know—

JOE: Situation.

CHARLIE AND FRANK: Situation.

CHARLIE: But now first things first. Who is bowling tonight?

FRANK: I'm in.

CHARLIE: And I'm in. Joey?

JOE: I told you, Charlie. I got all these things to do.

CHARLIE: You gonna let that bullshit get in your way? Are you forgetting who you are?

FRANK: Yeah, Joe. *Remember the crown jewels.*

JOE: You're right. Count me in.

CHARLIE: Great.

JOE: And *c'est la guerre!*

FRANK: But you know, Charlie, if you want to stay home and watch the Lindbergh movie tonight—we'll understand completely.

CHARLIE: Naah, I've seen it. Let's bowl.

FRANK: Okay.

JOE: Long as I'm home by midnight.

CHARLIE: What are you—Cinderella? (*sings*) "I'm the man who broke the bank at Monte Carlo."

(*They walk off along the girder. A bird sails by.*)

THE LIGHTS FADE

ENGLISH
MADE SIMPLE

English Made Simple was first presented at the Seattle Repertory Theatre in April 1994. The director was Bill Irwin, the set coordinator was Thomas Gregg Meyer, the lighting coordinator was Jay Strevey, the costume coordinator was Heather Doland, and the sound coordinator was David Pascal. The cast was as follows:

JILL	Liz McCarthy
JACK	R. Hamilton Wright
LOUDSPEAKER VOICE	John Aylward

(*Lights up on* JACK *and* JILL, *a pleasant young man and woman. He is holding a plastic drink glass and she a paper plate. They stand facing each other, frozen in place, several feet apart. In the background we hear the sounds of conversation, laughter, glasses clinking, etc.*)

LOUDSPEAKER VOICE: English Made Simple, Chapter Three. The party. Section One: Saying Hello.

JACK AND JILL: Hello! (*They take a step toward each other.*)

LOUDSPEAKER VOICE: But remember before you begin— (JACK AND JILL *stop.*) The first three minutes of conversation between two people can determine their relationship for the rest of eternity. (JACK *and* JILL *clear their throats in chorus, a bit nervously.*) So watch your language!

JACK: Hello.

JILL: Hi.

JACK: How are you?

JILL: Good.

JACK: I don't think I know you.

JILL: My name is Jill.

JACK: I'm Jack.

JACK AND JILL: How do you do.

JACK: Friend of the host?

JILL: Friend of the hostess.

JACK: Oh. So . . .

JILL: Well . . . (*Slight pause: a momentary loss for conversation.*)

JACK AND JILL: Nice party! (*They freeze.*)

LOUDSPEAKER VOICE: Excellent. But let's look at the underlying rhythm of this interchange. (JACK and JILL now repeat the interchange with exactly the same rhythm and expression as before.)

JACK: Ba–bump.

JILL: Beep.

JACK: Buh–buh–beep?

JILL: Boop.

JACK: Bee da dee da dump bop.

JILL: Da da da Bop.

JACK: Bop Bop.

JACK AND JILL: Ba da doo wop.

JACK: Bee dada beep?

JILL: Bee dada beep–beep.

JACK: Oh. Baaaa . . .

JILL: Booo . . . (Slight pause: a momentary loss for conversation.)

JACK AND JILL: Da wop bop!

JILL: Hello hello hello, it's always hello.

JACK: You are the most wonderful woman at this party.

JILL: And then good–bye good–bye.

JACK: You have a light that surrounds you.

JILL: Every time I hear the word "hello" it's like a magic incantation. An open sesame.

JACK: Hello, I say to her.

JILL: Abracadabra.

JACK: My name is Jack.

JILL: And I expect a whole new universe to open up in front of me, full of joy.

JACK: Hello hello.

JILL: And then good-bye good-bye. (*Jack and Jill freeze.*)

LOUDSPEAKER VOICE: Section Two. The Structure of English Conversation.

JILL: Fred!

LOUDSPEAKER VOICE: First name.

JACK: Mary!

LOUDSPEAKER VOICE: First name.

JACK AND JILL: Hello!

LOUDSPEAKER VOICE: Salutation. (JACK *and* JILL *kiss on the cheek.*) Social display of affection, followed by—

JILL: I didn't know you were here.

LOUDSPEAKER VOICE: Friendly observation, answered by—

JACK: I'm here.

LOUDSPEAKER VOICE: Statement of the obvious.

JILL: How are you?

LOUDSPEAKER VOICE: Superficial question about health.

JACK: Good.

LOUDSPEAKER VOICE: Superficial answer. Occupational question—

JACK: How's the job?

LOUDSPEAKER VOICE: And—

JILL: Terrific.

LOUDSPEAKER VOICE: Acceptable falsehood.

JACK: So . . .

LOUDSPEAKER VOICE: Meaningless monosyllable while searching for topic.

JILL: Quite a smorgasbord.

LOUDSPEAKER VOICE: Attempt at new topic.

JACK: Mmmmmmm.

LOUDSPEAKER VOICE: Noncommittal noise, to reject the topic. And—

JACK AND JILL: Well!

LOUDSPEAKER VOICE: Exclamation, to signal the approaching end of the interchange. Well done.

JACK: I was in love with you, once upon a time.

JILL: You asked me about my job, and I lied to you.

JACK: You who look so self-possessed and mature.

JILL: I would have answered you honestly, once upon a time.

JACK: Once upon a time you cried on my shoulder like a little child.

JILL: We would have talked like two people who love each other. Then we would have gone home and lain in bed.

JACK: We used to go to parties like this all the time.

JILL: Together.

JACK: So happy . . . (*Small pause.*)

JACK AND JILL: Well!

JILL: Nice seeing you, Fred. (*Kisses his cheek.*)

LOUDSPEAKER VOICE: Expression of pleasure. First name.

JACK: Take care of yourself, Mary.

LOUDSPEAKER VOICE: Parting wish. First name.

JACK AND JILL: 'Bye!

LOUDSPEAKER VOICE: Valediction. (JACK *and* JILL *freeze*.)

LOUDSPEAKER VOICE: Section Three. Simultaneous Translation, or: The secret meanings of common English words.

JILL: Well, well, well.

LOUDSPEAKER VOICE: In this context: "Oh, shit."

JACK: I didn't know you were here.

LOUDSPEAKER VOICE: "What the fuck are *you* doing here?"

JILL: How are you, Hank?

LOUDSPEAKER VOICE: "Wasn't five years enough?"

JACK: I'm good.

LOUDSPEAKER VOICE: "Fuck you, Agnes."

JILL: Nice party.

LOUDSPEAKER VOICE: "Asshole."

JACK : Very nice.

LOUDSPEAKER VOICE: "Fuck you, Agnes."

JILL: So what are you doing with yourself?

LOUDSPEAKER VOICE: "Are you still sleeping with that slut from the community college?"

JACK: Same old thing.

LOUDSPEAKER VOICE: "It's none of your fucking business."

JILL: Have you tried the chicken?

LOUDSPEAKER VOICE: "Have some salmonella?"

JACK: I'm sticking with liquids.

LOUDSPEAKER VOICE: "I know you have problems with your mother, but you don't have to *poison* me."

JILL: See you, Hank.

LOUDSPEAKER VOICE: "Up yours."

JACK: Take care.

LOUDSPEAKER VOICE: "Fuck you, Agnes."

JACK AND JILL: 'Bye! (*They freeze.*)

LOUDSPEAKER VOICE: Section Seven. Fill In The Blank, or: The arbitrariness of information. (*Note: In this section, each of the "possibilities"—e.g., "Jack, Bill, Ted," etc.—gets equal weight with the speaker. Each is a different "take" and equally true.*)

JACK: Excuse me, but don't I know you? My name is Jack.

JILL: Hello.

JACK: My name is Bill.

JILL: How are you.

JACK: My name is Ted.

JILL: How do you do.

JACK: Melvin. And you are . . . ?

JILL: Jill.

JACK: Hello, Jill.

JILL: Monica.

JACK: How are you, Monica.

JILL: Denise.

JACK: Could we have gone to college together?

JILL: I went to Stanford.

JACK: Ah.

JILL: Bennington.

JACK: Oh.

JILL: Chicago.

JACK: And—I'm sorry—your name is . . . ?

JILL: Louise. And you are?

JACK: Barney.

JILL: Where did you grow up, Bob?

JACK: Well . . .

JILL: Jim?

JACK: Well . . .

JILL: Stanley?

JACK: Well I grew up in Washington.

JILL: Oh.

JACK: St. Louis.

JILL: Great place.

JACK: Santa Fe.

JILL: Nice.

JACK: What about you, Jane?

JILL: My name is Jill.

JACK: I'm sorry. *Jill*.

JILL: And yet really my name could be anything. . . .

JACK: Anyway, I went to med school.

JILL: I wasn't born with a name.

JACK: Went to law school.

JILL: I was *given* a name.

JACK: Went to plumbing school.

JILL: My name could just as easily be Beth, or Phyllis, or Jane.

JACK: Quite a smorgasbord, isn't it?

JILL: Or Gertrude, or Natasha.

JACK: Do you know what the trouble with a smorgasbord is? There are too many choices.

JILL: A hummingbird doesn't have a name.

JACK: Do I want the chicken, or the roast beef?

JILL: A fish doesn't have a name.

JACK: Pâté, or cheese?

JILL: A hedgehog doesn't have a name.

JACK: It's just like life that way.

JILL: It's just this nameless *thing,* a handful of skin and fur and a heart beating inside it.

JACK: Should I work, should I read, should I listen to music?

JILL: Completely anonymous.

JACK: Should I go to this party, or should I go to the movies?

JILL: A hedgehog doesn't even know it doesn't have a name.

JACK: Sometimes there are so many choices, I don't do *anything!*

JILL: With a name you're just an example of something.

JACK: I thought to myself, this party could be a total waste.

JILL: But I'm not an example of something.

JACK: But I came to this party because I thought I might meet the love of my life.

JILL: I'm some *body*.

JACK: Do you think she's here?

JILL: I'm Jill.

JACK: I'm Jack.

JACK AND JILL: Hello. (*They freeze.*)

LOUDSPEAKER VOICE: Section Twenty-six. The Conditional Tense, or: Should, Would, Could.

JACK: Okay, so we meet at this party.

JILL: And we like each other.

JACK: We like each other instantly. (*Holds out hand.*) I'm Zeno.

JILL: Miranda.

(*They shake.*)

Did you know that the first three minutes of conversation can determine your relationship to the other person for all eternity?

JACK: But we pass the three-minute mark! We meet, and we mesh!

JILL: Oy, what a mesh.

JACK: And it all begins right here on this spot. In a single moment, all things seem possible.

JILL: All things *are* possible.

JACK: The infinite smorgasbord lies before us. But what do we do?

JILL: The party's wrapping up.

JACK: The crowd is thinning.

JILL: But the question of the moment is . . .

JACK: Do I ask you out?

JILL: Do *I* ask *you* out?

JACK: And if you do—

JACK AND JILL: Should I accept?

JACK: This could be one of those glorious and intoxicating meetings best left to memory.

JILL: Or it might be the start of eternal love.

JACK: So I say: Would you like to get a cup of coffee sometime? And you say—

JILL: Sorry. But thanks anyway.

JACK AND JILL: 'Bye!

JACK: And that's the road of no-thank-you.

JILL: A dead end.

JACK: But possibly a *happy* dead end. While down this road here, is . . .

JILL: Would you like to get a cup of coffee sometime?

JACK: Sure!

JILL: So we go out for coffee.

JACK: And we have a horrible time.

JILL: Dead end.

JACK: Or a wonderful time. In which case—

JILL: We get a second cup.

JACK: And stop right there.

JILL: Dead end.

JACK: Or we go out for a third cup and a fourth cup and a fifth cup.

JILL: Would we have made love by now?

JACK: Maybe we would have.

JILL: I say we should have.

JACK: We certainly *could* have.

JILL: Let's say we did.

JACK: And it was horrible.

JACK AND JILL: Dead end.

JILL: Or it was wonderful. Which means—

JACK: More coffee. And—

JILL: We move in with each other.

JACK: *Mistake*.

JILL: Dead end.

JACK: Or it could be wonderful!

JILL: And so we get engaged.

JACK: Marriage.

JILL: Children.

JACK: Bliss. (JACK *and* JILL *sigh blissfully*.)

JILL: And on to divorce.

JACK: Or—the other road—maybe we're down the road of no-thank-you we took years and years ago, and years and years pass.

JILL: And we meet each other at a party. And you say—

JACK: Hello, I'm Zeno.

JILL: Miranda.

JACK: Don't I know you from somewhere?

JILL: And a whole universe opens up in front of us—

JACK: Full of joy.

JILL: All things are possible.

JACK: And they start right on this spot.

JILL: Dead end.

JACK: Or bliss.

JILL: Should, would, could.

JACK: Well it was nice meeting you, Miranda.

JILL: Yes. Nice meeting you, Zeno. (*They reach their hands to shake, but freeze.*)

LOUDSPEAKER VOICE: Section Seventy-eight. Saying Good-bye.

JACK: Listen, I only have a few minutes.

LOUDSPEAKER VOICE: Let's practice a typical interchange.

JACK: The crowd is thinning and the party's wrapping up. Coats are disappearing from the pile on the bed. . . .

LOUDSPEAKER VOICE: A *typical* interchange, please!

JACK: I just wanted to say, while I have the chance, that you are the most wonderful woman at this party.

LOUDSPEAKER VOICE: *Typical,* please!

JACK: On this street. In this city. In the country. On this planet.

JILL: You're the most wonderful man I've met in years.

JACK: You have a light that surrounds you.

JILL: You're intoxicating.

JACK: You're radiant. I came to this party one thing and I leave it transformed.

JILL: I came to this party to meet the love of my life.

JACK: And you're her.

LOUDSPEAKER VOICE (*correcting*): You are *she*.

JACK: You're her! You are the love of my life!

JILL: My name could be anything.

JACK: But it's Jill.

JILL: I could have gone anywhere tonight.

JACK: But you came to this party.

JILL: Hello hello.

JACK: Abracadabra. My name is Jack.

JILL: Would you like to get a cup of coffee sometime, Jack?

JACK: Yes, Jill, I would like that very much.

JILL: And it all happens right here.

LOUDSPEAKER VOICE: A-plus.

BLACKOUT

A

SINGULAR
KINDA GUY

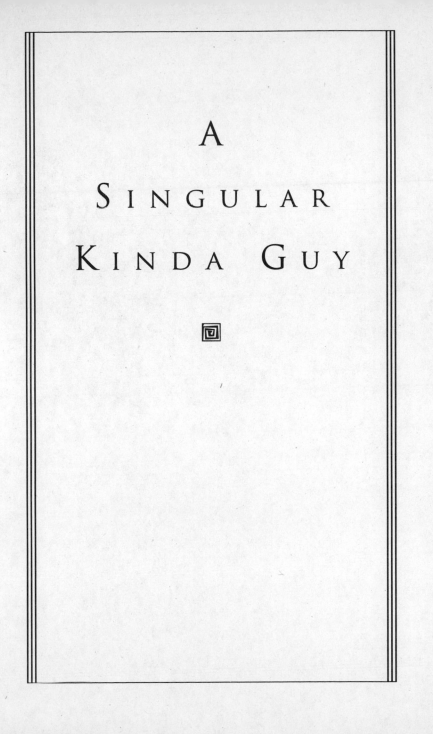

Lights up on MITCH, *a guy out on a Saturday night.*

A young guy is out on a Saturday night in his best shoes, talking to a girl he's met in a bar. She's nice, he likes her. But he's got this sort of confession, see. There's something she ought to know about him. And he's never told this to anybody. You see, on the inside, deep on the inside, he isn't really a guy at all. He's an Olivetti electric self-correcting typewriter. And he can't even type!

MITCH: I know what you're thinking. You're looking at me and you're saying to yourself, Average guy. Normal human being. Nothing out of the ordinary. Well, that's what I thought too for lots of years, and boy, was I wrong. Now I look back, I think I always really knew the truth about myself, underneath. It's like, sometimes I'd look in the mirror in the morning and I'd get this weird feeling like what I was looking at was not what I really was looking at. Or else I'd be standing in a crowd of people at a party, and suddenly I'd get this idea like I was standing in a huge empty space and there wasn't anybody around me for miles. Episodes of "vastation," if you know that beautiful word. And then one day I had a . . . I don't know what you'd call it. A mystical experience?

I was walking down Lex over in the Thirties when I go by this office supply shop. Just a crummy little place. But I turn and I look and I see . . . an Olivetti Model 250 portable electric typewriter. Are you familiar with that particular model? Have you ever seen the old Olivetti 250? Well let me tell you—it is sublime. The lines. The shape. The slant of the keyboard. It's all there! It's a thing of beauty!

Anyway, I'm standing there looking at this thing, and it's like I recognize it from someplace. It's like I'm looking at family somehow, like I'm seeing some long-lost older

brother for the first time, and suddenly I realize—*That's me,*
right there. That thing in the window is exactly what I feel
like, on the inside. Same lines, same shape, same aesthetic.
And what I realized was—I am a typewriter. No, really! A
typewriter! All those years I thought I was a human being,
on the inside I was really a portable Olivetti 250 with auto-
matic correctability. And you know what? I can't even type!

Needless to say, this revelation came as a shock. But all of
a sudden it's clear to me how come I always got off on big
words—like "vastation." Or "phenomenological." Or
"subcutaneous." Words are what a typewriter's all about,
right?

Problem is, it can be a lonely thing, being a typewriter in
a world of human beings. And now here I am being replaced
every day by word processors. Who needs a typewriter anymore? Here I finally figure out what I really am, I'm an
antique already.

Plus, there's my love life, which is problematical to say
the least. The difficulties involved in a typewriter finding a
suitable partner in this town are fairly prodigious, as you
can imagine. At least now I know how come I always
loved—not just sex, sex is anywhere—but . . . touch.
Being touched, and touching. Being touched is part of the
nature and purpose of typewriters, that's how we express
ourselves and the human person along with us. Hands on
the keyboard and the right touch—fire away. Yeah
women's hands. They're practically the first thing I notice.
Nice set of shapely fingers. Good manicure. No hangnails.
Soft skin. I'm not a finger fetishist or anything, you understand, it's just . . .

You've got a pretty nice pair of hands yourself, there.
That's what I noticed, that's how come I stepped over here
to talk to you. I know this all sounds pretty loony, but you
know I've never told anybody this before? Somehow I just
felt like I could trust you, and . . .

What? I beg your pardon?

I don't understand.

You're not really a girl? Sure, you're a girl, you're a beautiful girl, so . . .

You're what? You're actually a sheet of paper? Ten-pound bond? Ivory tinted? Pure cotton fiber? (MITCH *holds out his hand*.) Glad to meet you.

BLACKOUT

SPEED-THE-PLAY

*This play is for Martha Stoberock,
with love, because it made her laugh,
and just because*

Speed-the-Play was performed at the Mitzi Newhouse Theater at Lincoln Center on November 20, 1989, as part of a benefit for Broadway Cares, hosted by *Spy* magazine and honoring David Mamet. The evening was directed by Gregory Mosher, and the cast was as follows:

American Buffalo

DONNY	J. J. Johnston
BOBBY	W. H. Macy
TEACH	Mike Nussbaum

Speed-the-Plow

GOULD	Joe Mantegna
FOX	Bob Balaban
KAREN	Felicity Huffman

Sexual Perversity in Chicago

BERNIE	Treat Williams
DANNY	Steven Goldstein
DEBORAH	Mariel Hemingway
JOAN	Felicity Huffman

Glengarry Glen Ross

LEVENE	Robert Prosky
WILLIAMSON	W. H. Macy
MOSS	J. J. Johnston
AARONOW	Mike Nussbaum
ROMA	Joe Mantegna
CUSTOMER	Steven Goldstein

M.C.	Roderick McLachlan

Lights up on the M.C. *at a podium.*

M.C.: David Mamet. Poker player. Cigar smoker. Male bonder. Winner of the Pulitzer Prize. Film director. Chicagoan. *Genius.* Why is David Mamet a genius? Because from a very early age, he instinctively knew three important things about his audience. First—Americans like speed. Things that are fast. This is, after all, the country that invented the rock song and the roller coaster, and might have invented premature ejaculation if it hadn't been invented already. So Mamet keeps his plays in fifth gear. Second—David Mamet knows that Americans don't like to pay for parking. So he keeps his plays short. Third—he knows how Americans talk. Particularly American men. He appreciates that when American men go to the theater, they want to hear familiar words like "asshole" and "jagoff." Which might explain the popularity of *American Buffalo,* in which the word "fuck" appears over sixteen thousand times. We are gathered here tonight to honor David Mamet for his contribution to the American theater. Some of you might not be familiar with the Master's work, so we have, as it were, boiled down a few of the major plays and extracted the gist, to give you the Master's *oovruh* in the Master's own way: short, and to the fuckin' *point.* Four plays in seven minutes. You are about to enter . . . the Mamet Zone. (*He rings a fight bell.*) *American Buffalo.* Act One. A junkshop. (DANNY *and* BOBBY *enter.*)

DANNY: Bobby, you're a young punk.

BOBBY: Fuckin' right I am.

DANNY: A small-time thief.

BOBBY: Fuckin' right I am.

DANNY: But we never use the word "thief," do we, Bobby?

BOBBY: Fuckin' right we don't.

DANNY: And do you fence stolen goods through my junk shop?

BOBBY: We never talk about it.

DANNY: Fuckin' right we don't.

BOBBY: So what do we talk about, Danny?

DANNY: The nature of life. We also say "fuck" a lot. (TEACH *enters*.)

TEACH: Fuckin' *life*.

DANNY: Is it bad, Teach?

TEACH: It's very bad.

DANNY: Go for more coffee, Bob. (BOBBY *exits*.)

TEACH: Fuckin' Fletcher. Fuckin' Ruthie.

DANNY: You ran into Ruthie heretofore?

TEACH: I'm over in the coffee shop puttin' my finger on the Zeitgeist, Ruthie's sittin' there talkin' objective correlatives. "Bull*shit,*" I say. Next thing I know, form follows content, this fuckin' cunt is traveling around the corner with my *sweet*roll! For which I paid for, sixty-fi' *cents* plus a truckload of stolen pig iron. Now is that the mirror back to nature, or what? As for fuckin' I-don't-*give*-a-shit-what-anybody-says *Fletcher,* I say the guy is a hairdresser, and I only hope some vicious lesbo with a zipgun rips his fuckin' lips off. (*Pause.*) What's new?

DANNY: Not much. I was thinkin' I'd ask Bobby to steal some rare coins for me tonight.

TEACH: Maybe I should do it instead.

DANNY: Okay.

(*Bell.*)

M.C.: Act Two. The junkshop, that night. (TEACH *and* DANNY *enter.*)

TEACH: Everything's fucked up, Danny. I can't steal the rare coins.

DANNY: I fear I detect a rationalization, Teach.

TEACH: Why don't you go take a leak in the gene pool you swam in on. (BOBBY *enters.*)

BOBBY: Hey, Danny. Want to buy this rare buffalo-head nickel?

TEACH: Fuck you, Bobby. (*He hits* BOBBY *with a pigsticker.*)

BOBBY: *OW!*

DANNY: Fuck you, Teach.

TEACH: Fuck you, Danny.

BOBBY: Fuck you, Danny and Teach. (*Pause.*)

TEACH: So is there anything more to say?

(*Three bells.*)

M.C.: *Speed-the-Plow.* Act One. An office in Hollywood.

(*Bell.* FOX *and* GOULD *enter.*)

FOX: Gould, you are the new head of production at this studio.

GOULD: I am.

FOX: I am an unsuccessful independent producer.

GOULD: You are.

FOX: And you owe me a favor.

GOULD: Forsooth?

FOX: I own this piece-a-shit movie script. Will you take it to the head of the studio and make me rich?

GOULD: I'll do it at ten o'clock tomorrow morning.

FOX: Thank you, Gould.

GOULD: I'm a whore.

FOX: I'm a whore too.

GOULD: And we're *men.*

FOX: Who's the sexy new secretary?

GOULD: Some fuckin' temp.

FOX: I bet you five hundred bills you can't get her in the sack.

GOULD: It's a bet. (*Into intercom.*) Karen, would you come in here, please? (KAREN *enters.*)

KAREN: Sir?

GOULD: Karen, would you read this book about cosmic bullshit that somebody submitted and come to my house tonight to report on it?

KAREN: Yes sir. (*She exits.*)

GOULD: Consider her fucked.

(*Bell.*)

M.C.: Act Two. Gould's house, that evening.

(GOULD *and* KAREN *enter.*)

GOULD: Did you read the book about cosmic bullshit, Karen?

KAREN: Yes and I think the book is brilliant.

GOULD: It might be.

KAREN: And Mr. Fox's script is trash.

GOULD: It may be.

KAREN: So why will you produce it?

GOULD: Because I'm a whore.

KAREN: *I* think you're a very sensitive man. (*Small pause.*)

GOULD: At last a girl who understands me! (*They embrace.*)

(*Bell.*)

M.C.: Act Three. Gould's office, the next morning. (GOULD *and* FOX *enter.*)

GOULD: I'm not gonna recommend your script, Fox.

FOX: No?

GOULD: I'm not going to the head of the studio with it.

FOX: No?

GOULD: I'm gonna recommend this brilliant book on cosmic bullshit instead. Why? Because the business of America is Byzantine.

FOX: You lift your leg to pee.

GOULD: You genuflect to pick your nose.

FOX: You stand on your head to jerk off.

GOULD: You bounce on a trampoline to defecate.

FOX: You know you're only doing this because that shtupka fired off a twenty-one-gun salute on your weenie. (*Small pause.*)

GOULD: You're right. (*Into intercom.*) Karen, would you come in here, please? (KAREN *enters.*)

KAREN: Bob . . . Bob . . . Bob . . .

GOULD: You're fired. (KAREN *exits.*)

FOX: She's a whore.

GOULD: She's a whore.

FOX: And you're my friend.

GOULD: If only we were women, we could be lesbians together.

FOX: But in the meantime, life—

GOULD: —is very good.

(*Three bells.*)

M.C.: *Sexual Perversity in Chicago.* Scene One. A singles bar.

(*Bell.* DANNY *and* BERNIE *enter.*)

BERNIE: All women are alike, Danny.

DANNY: Gosh, Bernie. Is that really true?

BERNIE: Essentially they're bitches.

DANNY: Or else they're whores?

BERNIE: Yes. Or else they're whores.

(*Bell.*)

M.C.: Scene Two. Joan and Deborah's apartment. (JOAN *and* DEBORAH *enter.*)

JOAN: All men are alike, Deborah.

DEBORAH: They certainly are, Joan.

JOAN AND DEBORAH: They're *men*.

(*Bell.*)

M.C.: Scene Three. A singles bar. (JOAN, *alone.* BERNIE *enters.*)

BERNIE: Hi there.

JOAN: Get lost.

BERNIE: You got a lotta fuckin' *nerve.*

(*Bell.*)

M.C.: Scene Four. A library. (DEBORAH, *alone.* DANNY *enters.*)

DANNY: Hi there.

DEBORAH: Get lost.

DANNY: Want to go out with me?

DEBORAH: Okay.

(*Bell.*)

M.C.: Scene Five. Bernie's apartment. (BERNIE, *alone.*)

BERNIE: Is there a metaphysical point to broads?

(*Bell.*)

M.C.: Scene Six. Danny's apartment. (DANNY *and* DEBORAH *in bed.*)

DANNY: Nice nice, Deborah.

DEBORAH: Nice nice, Danny.

DANNY AND DEBORAH: Good-night! (*They fall asleep.*)

(*Bell.*)

M.C.: Scene Seven. A bar. (DANNY, DEBORAH *and* BERNIE.)

DANNY (*introducing*): Bernie, Deborah. Deborah, Bernie.

DEBORAH AND BERNIE: Hello!

BERNIE: You sure are a nice girl, Deborah. (*Aside to* DANNY.) Probably a whore.

(*Bell.*)

M.C.: Scene Eight. Danny and Bernie's office.

BERNIE: Danny, people sometimes have sexual intercourse under very peculiar circumstances.

DANNY: Is that true, Bernie?

BERNIE: Yes it is.

(*Bell.*)

M.C.: Scene Nine. Deborah and Joan's apartment. (JOAN *and* DEBORAH *enter.*)

JOAN: Is there a metaphysical point to men? (DEBORAH *is about to answer when she is interrupted by . . . the bell.*)

M.C.: Scene Ten. An office.

BERNIE: Don't fall in love, Danny.

DANNY: Mmn.

BERNIE: Deborah's just another bitch.

DANNY: Mmn.

BERNIE: I gather that you don't agree?

(*Bell.*)

M.C.: Scene Eleven. Danny's apartment. (DANNY *and* DEBORAH *in bed.*)

DANNY: Breast.

DEBORAH: Sperm.

DANNY: Penis.

DEBORAH: Menstruation.

DANNY: Masturbation.

DEBORAH: Your come smells just like Clorox.

DANNY: I think I'm falling in love with you.

M.C.: He does so.

(*Bell.*)

M.C. Scene Twelve. A toy shop. (DANNY *and* BERNIE *enter.*)

BERNIE: When I was a child, an old man once placed his hand on my genitals in a movie theater.

DANNY: On your genitals?

BERNIE: In a movie theater.

DANNY: Was it psychologically damaging?

BERNIE: How do I know, Danny? I was only a fucking *child*.

(*Bell.*)

M.C.: Scene Thirteen. A restaurant. (DEBORAH *and* JOAN *enter.*)

DEBORAH: I'm going to move in with Danny. (JOAN *puts a finger down her throat and gags.*)

(*Bell.*)

M.C.: Scene Fourteen. The office. (BERNIE *and* DANNY.)

BERNIE: Ba deep ba dop ba *doop,* Dan.

DANNY: I know that, Bernie.

BERNIE: Da-da-daaa some girl, da-da-daaa it's love, da-da-daaa you're fucked. Oop scoop a wee-bop, bonk, *deek!*

DANNY: Sure, I see your point.

(*Bell.*)

M.C.: Scene Fifteen. Danny and Deborah's apartment. (DANNY *and* DEBORAH *enter.*)

DANNY: Where's the shampoo?

DEBORAH: Will you still love me when I'm old?

DANNY: Why are you putting on dirty panty hose?

DEBORAH: Are we all right?

DANNY: Bitch.

DEBORAH: Jerk. I'm moving out.

(*Bell.*)

M.C.: Scene Sixteen. Deborah and Joan's apartment. (DEBORAH *and* JOAN *enter.*)

JOAN: All men are alike, Deborah.

DEBORAH: Oh be quiet.

(*Bell.*)

M.C.: Scene Seventeen. A beach. (DANNY *and* BERNIE *enter.*)

DANNY: All women are alike, Bernie.

BERNIE: Yes, they are.

DANNY: They're bitches.

BERNIE: Or else they're whores. And life, Danny boy?

DANNY: Life is good, Bernie.

BERNIE: Yes, life is *very* good.

(*Three bells.*)

M.C.: *Glengarry Glen Ross.* Act One, Scene One. A booth in a Chinese restaurant.

(LEVENE *and* WILLIAMSON *in a booth.*)

LEVENE: John. John. John. Forty, fifty, sixty years I been the best goddamn hustler of swampland in the history of real estate. I started selling real estate before I was *born. I* hit the calls. *I* caught the marks. *I* platted out the stats. I ate the chalk. I made the fuckin' *board,* John.

WILLIAMSON: Uh-huh.

LEVENE: Now I wanna win that Cadillac as top salesman of the month, I need some leads.

WILLIAMSON: You can't have any leads, Shelley.

LEVENE: Oh *please,* John, *please?*

(*Bell.*)

M.C.: Scene Two. Another booth at the restaurant. (MOSS *and* AARONOW *in the booth*.)

MOSS: We're gonna win that fuckin' Cadillac, Aaronow.

AARONOW: *Duhhh.*

MOSS: You and me. Know how?

AARONOW: *Duhhh.*

MOSS: We're gonna steal the leads from the office.

AARONOW: *Duhhh.*

MOSS: I mean you and me, Aaronow. To*night.*

AARONOW: Wouldn't that be illegal?

(*Bell.*)

M.C.: Scene Three. Another booth at the restaurant. (ROMA *and a* POTENTIAL CUSTOMER.)

ROMA: What is the meaning of life?

POTENTIAL CUSTOMER: I don't know.

ROMA: Me either. Would you like to buy some real estate?

(*Bell.*)

M.C.: Act Two. The real-estate office, the next morning. (WILLIAMSON, MOSS, AARONOW *and* ROMA *with a* POLICEMAN.)

WILLIAMSON: Somebody broke into the office last night and stole the leads. Was it you, Moss?

MOSS: I ain't talkin'.

WILLIAMSON: Was it you, Roma?

ROMA: Suck my dick.

WILLIAMSON: Was it you, Aaronow?

AARONOW: *Duhhh.* (LEVENE *enters.*)

LEVENE: Hand over the Cadillac! I just made a sale!

WILLIAMSON: Sorry, Levene. *You* were the one who stole the leads last night. (*To* POLICEMAN.) Take Levene away.

LEVENE: You can't take me away! I made the calls! I hit the board! I won the car! You can't do this!

WILLIAMSON: Yes I can. We're illustrating the nature of American capitalism.

LEVENE: Oh. Okay. (POLICEMAN *takes him away*.)

AARONOW: Can I have a Cadillac?

WILLIAMSON: No.

ROMA: Is there anybody here who hasn't said "fuck"? (*Small pause.*) I'll be at the restaurant.

BLACKOUT

ANCIENT HISTORY

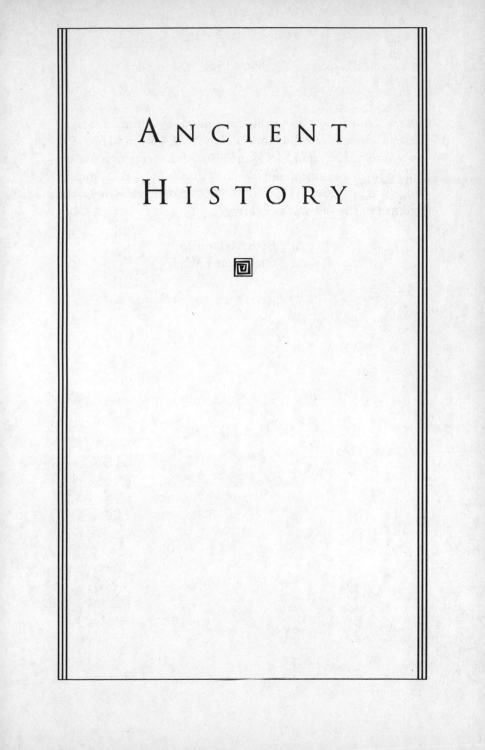

Ancient History was originally presented by Primary Stages (Casey Childs, artistic director) in New York City in May 1989. It was directed by Jason McConnell Buzas; the set design was by Philipp Jung; costume design was by Claudia Stephens; lighting design was by Deborah Constantine; sound design was by David Ferdinand. The cast was as follows:

RUTH   Beth McDonald
JACK   Christopher Wells

ACT ONE

Dark stage. Silence.

RUTH'S VOICE: Paradise.

JACK'S VOICE: Absolutely.

(*We hear the duet "Au fond du temple saint" from Bizet's* The Pearl Fishers *in the distance, as the lights come up on* RUTH's *bedroom: a bed, a mirror, a clock, a telephone, a door to the outside, and a door to a bathroom. Some clothing scattered around the room.* RUTH *and* JACK *are lying together on the rumpled bed. They are in their mid-thirties. She is wearing a brightly figured robe. He, a plain white robe.*)

RUTH: Paradise.

JACK: Absolutely.

RUTH: Paradise.

JACK: Absolutely. (*Sighs contentedly.*)

RUTH: This is what I call *shayn* [i.e., beautiful].

JACK: This is what I call *molto* shayn.

RUTH: They ought to put us on TV.

JACK: Or bottle us.

RUTH: The world would be littered with empties.

JACK: Can you imagine what the world would be like if everybody lived like this?

RUTH: It'd be utopia.

JACK: Earthly paradise.

RUTH: Absolutely.

JACK: There'd be no more war. No strife.

RUTH: No hunger.

JACK: No hatred.

RUTH: No Pekingeses.

JACK: All dogs would die of hunger because their owners would be in bed all the time.

RUTH: No cats, either.

JACK: No Siamese cats, anyway.

RUTH: No cats of any stripe.

JACK: No toupées.

RUTH: No German novels.

JACK: No chewing gum.

RUTH: No Sunday-afternoon football on TV.

JACK: Hey. Don't knock football.

RUTH: All right. We'll keep football.

JACK: You don't understand its subtleties.

RUTH: No cigars.

JACK: No houseplants.

RUTH: No polyester.

JACK: No parents.

RUTH: No polyester.

JACK: No parents.

RUTH: No polyester . . .

JACK: No parents . . .

(*Small pause.*)

RUTH: No canned spaghetti.

JACK: No men who wear fur coats.

RUTH: No fat women who wear short dresses.

JACK: No Jehovah's Witnesses waking you up on Sunday morning for a contribution.

RUTH: No Jews on street corners saying "Are you Jewish?" only to the men.

JACK: No religion of any slant.

RUTH: No political parties.

JACK: No international boundaries.

RUTH: No extraterrestrial boundaries.

JACK: No time.

RUTH: No space.

JACK: No matter.

RUTH: No antimatter.

JACK: God, isn't it simple?

RUTH: Yeah. Utopia's a snap when you get right down to it.

JACK: *Es ist ganz einfach.* [It's perfectly simple.]

(*Pause.*)

RUTH: Only what's left? I mean, when you take all those things away.

JACK: *Shtupping* [i.e., fucking]. *Shtupping* with just the right English on it.

RUTH: No former girlfriends, either.

JACK: *Or* boyfriends.

RUTH: Or ex-wives.

JACK: No talking about them, anyway.

RUTH: Maybe you'd be given a drug after every relationship that'd make you forget all about them.

JACK: So you could start afresh.

RUTH: Yeah. A virgin all over again.

JACK: A version all over again.

RUTH: Aversion? As in therapy?

JACK: No, as in every man wants to marry a version. Of something.

RUTH (*"I'm impressed"*): Oooooooh.

JACK: I am a clever child.

RUTH: And aren't we the most discriminating and tasteful couple you ever saw?

JACK: *We'd* know how to put a world together. How come they never asked us?

RUTH: Yeah, how come they never consulted the experts?

JACK: The fools.

RUTH: Now let's never move, Pinky.

JACK: All right.

RUTH: Ever.

JACK: Pinky—it's a deal. (*Small pause.*) Except you're on my leg. . . .

RUTH: Oh, sorry.

JACK: No, don't move. I always wanted gangrene. As an experience.

(The phone rings and they suddenly go completely still. The lights change slightly, darkening. Then the phone rings once again, the lights return to where they'd been, and the two go on exactly as they had before.)

RUTH: Aren't we the most discriminating and tasteful couple you ever saw?

JACK: *We'd* know how to put a world together. How come they never asked us?

RUTH: *And no varicose veins.*

JACK: I beg your pardon?

RUTH: In our perfect world. No varicose veins.

JACK: Alas, varicose veins are inevitable.

RUTH: They're disgusting.

JACK: You can get rid of Pekingeses and polyester, but varicose veins are part of the grand design.

RUTH: Would you still love me if I had varicose veins?

JACK: Of course not.

RUTH: Would it be all over?

JACK: It would be *all over.*

RUTH: Somehow I thought so. But you know you're not supposed to say things like that on my birthday.

JACK *(an old routine between them)*: What? I'm *not?*

RUTH AND JACK *(together)*: *Uh-oh!*

JACK: Anyway you're not going to get them. Varicose veins, I mean.

RUTH: Can we get off varicose veins?

JACK: An ugly blue bulging vein ruin those gorgeous gams? No sirree, I'd never allow it. In fact—let me kiss those perfect gams right now. (*He starts to kiss his way up her leg.*)

RUTH: Jack! No!

JACK: Yes! I must! I pine for your kneecaps!

RUTH: Jack, stop that! Come back!

JACK: No, I must kiss your legs, I— (*Stops abruptly, making a face.*)

RUTH: What's the matter?

JACK: Nothing. Just a small case of crabs.

RUTH: Oh *stop*.

JACK: Minor infestation of pubic lice. Nothing to worry about.

RUTH: Oh God, stop it!

JACK: Let me pick one off.

RUTH: Will you *stop?*

JACK: Mmm! Delicious!

RUTH: Jack—

JACK: You crack them in your teeth, like pistachios.

RUTH: You're disgusting.

JACK: Dig out the meaty part. Yum yum.

RUTH: Get back up here. Come on. (*She pulls him back by her side.*)

JACK: Have I ever told you about spending my thirtieth birthday picking nits out of my girlfriend's pubic hair?

RUTH: About a hundred times.

JACK: Do I repeat myself? Very well then, I repeat myself.

RUTH: I tell you, when we get our perfect world . . .

JACK: I know. There'll be no crabs.

RUTH: I don't care about the crabs so much. You just couldn't *talk* about them all the time.

JACK: But we're adults. We're twentieth-century grown-ups. We can talk about anything.

RUTH: Not for the twentieth time. Do you remember how somebody once said "Hell is other people"?

JACK: Yeah. J. P. Sartre.

RUTH: Hell isn't other people. It's other people telling the same story for the twentieth time.

JACK: And do you know what *that* is?

RUTH: What.

JACK AND RUTH (*together*): *Marriage.*

RUTH: Ah! Now we are onto marriage, and ready for blastoff.

JACK: It's in the dictionary. "Marriage. Archaic noun. Two people telling each other the same story for the twentieth time."

RUTH: Thank you!

JACK: Have I ever told you about spending my thirtieth birthday picking nits out of my girlfriend's pubic hair?

RUTH: Who was she, anyway?

JACK: I thought you didn't want to talk about it.

RUTH: I don't think I really want to know.

JACK: Good.

RUTH: Was she as good-looking as me?

JACK: No.

RUTH: That's all right, then. But speaking of birthdays . . .

JACK: Birthdays? Birthdays?

RUTH: Yeah. Do I get my presents now?

JACK: Sorry, Pinky. No presents till after the guests leave.

RUTH: Pleeeeeeeeease, Pinky?

JACK: Oh all right. One present.

RUTH: Great.

JACK: The rest you'll get after the party. Sixteen *million* frisky sperms.

RUTH: So what did you get me? Huh? Whadja get me?

JACK: Well you know they've started issuing the complete trombone suites of Arthur Honegger. In seven volumes?

RUTH: Mm-hm . . . ?

JACK: And I know how much you love Honegger.

RUTH: Honegger, off-egger.

JACK: Oh, very good! Ten points!

RUTH: *Sechel.* (*Pronounced "sayk'l."*)

JACK: What's that, Jewish pastry?

RUTH: Jewish brains.

JACK: Oh you are such a clever people, thinking up words like sechel, and Schlegel, and bagel.

RUTH: But to tell you the honest-to-God truth, I didn't really want the complete Honegger trombone suites.

JACK: What? You *didn't??*

JACK AND RUTH: *Uh-oh!*

JACK: What *did* you want?

RUTH: What did you get me and I'll tell you.

JACK: You have to guess.

RUTH: I don't want to guess. Just hand over the loot, will ya?

JACK (*takes a small box from under the bed*): Say "antidisestablish-mentarianism."

RUTH: Antidisestablishmentarianism.

JACK: Happy birthday. (*He hands it over.*)

RUTH (*tearing off the gift-wrapping*): Oh God I love presents. I love presents. . . .

JACK: A bottle of Kwell, what a perfect idea.

RUTH: I'm not even going to ask what Kwell is.

JACK: Kills pubic lice instantly.

RUTH: I should've known. (*She sees what's inside the box.*) Oh, Pinky! A pair of Droopy Eyes! (*It's a pair of trick glasses—the kind in which the eyes hang out of the frames on long springs.*) How did you know? (*She puts them on.*)

JACK: I thought you'd want them to go with your Norma Kamali dress.

RUTH: Gosh, thanks, Pinky.

JACK: Anything for you, Pinky. (*Kiss.*)

RUTH: If the rest of the presents are like this, I'm going to kill you.

JACK: Would it be all over?

RUTH: It would be *all over.*

JACK: All right, then, greedy bitch. Just to assuage your insatiable rapaciosity.

RUTH: Rapaciositudinousness.

JACK: Try this. (*He takes a larger box from under the bed.*)

RUTH: You shouldn't have.

JACK: But I did.

RUTH: But you shouldn't have.

JACK: But I did. Now open it.

RUTH: I thought you'd never ask. (*She tears open the box.*) Oh God, Jack . . .

JACK: Do you like it?

RUTH: Oh *God* . . . ! (RUTH *has taken a silk kimono out of the box.*)

JACK: God? Who? No such entity. The invention of a lot of silly superstitious cave-dwellers.

RUTH: It's incredible!

JACK: So what do you expect from tall, thin and tasteful people?

RUTH: But how could you afford this?

JACK: Oh, I sold a couple more quarts down at the blood bank. (RUTH *puts it on and looks in the mirror.*) You should put the Droopy Eyes on with that. It was meant as an ensemble.

RUTH: Is it gorgeous?

JACK: It's very gorgeous.

RUTH: Can I attack you?

JACK: Attack me. Make my body your bombing target. (*He opens his arms wide and she jumps into them. They fall onto the bed together.*) Yes! Yes! More sex, you lusty wench! (RUTH *lies back blissfully and sighs.*)

RUTH: Oh God I'm happy!

JACK: I thought you were attacking me. What happened?

RUTH: I don't think I've ever been as happy as I am right now.

JACK: Actually you've been exactly this happy in the arms of half a dozen men. You've just forgotten.

RUTH: Oh shut up.

JACK: Just as you'll forget me some day.

RUTH: Don't spoil it. Cynic.

JACK: Pollyanna.

RUTH: Fatalist.

JACK: Running dog of bourgeois optimism.

RUTH: You're wonderful.

JACK: Speak for yourself. (*Long kiss. They lie back on the pillows.*)

RUTH: Paradise.

JACK: Absolutely.

RUTH: This is what I call shayn.

JACK: "Shayn! Come back!"

RUTH: God, it's crazy.

JACK: Everything's crazy.

RUTH: I mean it's ironic.

JACK: Everything's ironic, if you look at it the right way. Anyway, what's crazy and ironic today?

RUTH: I was just thinking how this guy pursued me for months and months and I never went to bed with him, and then I saw you *twice* and *I* paid for both of the movies, and bang! Ten days that shook the bed.

JACK: Who was this?

RUTH: Just a guy.

JACK: Right before you started going out with me?

RUTH: Uh-huh.

JACK: And he pursued you for months and you never went to bed with him?

RUTH: Two months, three months, something like that.

JACK: *Three months without sex?* Who carries on a platonic relationship for three months anymore, even in these days of the great viruses?

RUTH: Hey. It wasn't *entirely* platonic.

JACK: Oh. (*Pause.*) How far'd he get?

RUTH: What?

JACK: How far did he get? I mean, if he didn't get to bed with you.

RUTH: What do you want, sixteen-millimeter films?

JACK: I'm just curious. First base? Second base? Shortstop?

RUTH: Shortstop?

JACK: Yeah.

RUTH: What's shortstop?

JACK: You know what shortstop is.

RUTH: I never went to an all-boys Catholic school.

JACK: That's when she lets you work her through her panties but won't let you put your hand inside.

RUTH: Where have I been all these years?

JACK: I guess you were educated wrong.

RUTH: I guess I was.

JACK: Then after you round third you come sliding into home, and—

RUTH: I think I understand the system, thank you.

JACK: Good. (*Slight pause.*) So did he get to third base?

RUTH: Jack, he wasn't even interesting!

JACK: But did he get to third base?

RUTH: No. We got called on account of rain. Is there anything but sex for you?

JACK: Nope. Freud was right. Everything is sex.

RUTH: Yeah? What about love?

JACK: Love? Love?

RUTH: Yeah, remember love?

JACK: That hormonal scam? The greatest con-job since Christianity.

RUTH: Rather an important factor in the world, bub.

JACK: No. *I'll* tell you what's important in the world.

RUTH: Tell me what's important.

JACK: *Like.* And like*ness.* People who like the same things and are alike. Two people in a bed who really *like* each other. Forget all your prophets preaching love. In an ideal world, there'd be *like* songs, and volumes of *like* poetry.

RUTH: So even in utopia there'd be no love?

JACK: I'd have it confiscated at the border.

RUTH: You don't really mean that.

JACK: I absolutely mean that.

RUTH: Well I'm sorry but I beg to differ.

JACK: You really think there'd be love in utopia? After all the damage it's done to the world?

RUTH: *Especially* in utopia there'd be love.

JACK: Why. State your case succinctly and give examples.

RUTH: Well . . .

JACK: Yes?

RUTH: Give me a second here.

JACK: I'd love to hear the case for love.

RUTH: Well in utopia you're supposed to be safe, right? I mean, you're supposed to be protected in utopia.

JACK: Yeah, and—?

RUTH: And that's what love makes you feel.

JACK: Safe?

RUTH: More than safe. Invulnerable. Like nothing could touch you. Like you're protected against death and sickness and unhappiness and the ravages of time and the dog at the door.

JACK: I thought love was supposed to make you feel vulnerable.

RUTH: No, getting *dumped* makes you feel vulnerable. Not falling in love.

JACK: Well I'll go for intense *like*. And intense alikeness. *Gleich mit gleich gesellt sich gern.*

RUTH: Translate, please!

JACK: Like with like goes gladly.

RUTH: Into English, I mean.

JACK: Similar things and people go together naturally.

RUTH: Sounds like something the Germans would say.

JACK: Oops.

RUTH: A nation of potato people. *Nazi* potato people. And very, very unfunny.

JACK: My great-grandmother was German.

RUTH: Was she funny?

JACK: Not really.

RUTH: I rest my case.

JACK: She did leave me a very beautiful brass bed.

RUTH: Melted down from brass knuckles, no doubt.

JACK: No, no—I loved that bed.

RUTH: Uh—*loved* it?

JACK: Intensely liked it.

RUTH: Thank you.

(*Lights begin to wash out.*)

JACK: God I had some wonderful nights in my youth, jingling the brass on that bed. *Après le déluge* Joan got it, of course.

RUTH: Hell isn't other people. . . .

JACK: Now she's off somewhere jingling other men, on my brass bed.

RUTH: Hell is remembering other people. . . .

JACK: And such are the thoughts that keep me awake a-nights.

(*Small pause, as the lights return to where they were before that section.*)

RUTH: Did you know that there's a slight touch of green in your complexion?

JACK: Yeah. I used to go out with a Chinese girl and when we stood close together we looked blue. That's color theory.

RUTH: Oh what a clever child it is.

JACK: I am a clever little boy.

RUTH: Pinky—what do you say we do this forever. Don't you think we could? I mean—

JACK: Do this forever?

RUTH: Yeah. I mean, doesn't this make you think—

JACK: What.

RUTH: Nothing.

JACK: Doesn't it make me think I could reconsider my usual dark and nasty ideas about the abominable institution of marriage?

RUTH: Something like that.

JACK: Doesn't this make me think I could find marriage less than asphyxiating?

RUTH: Something like that.

JACK: And terminally dull.

RUTH: Something along those lines.

JACK: And that children are not the ultimate horror, designed by some maleficent deity to scream in your ear, shit in your hand, and bankrupt you?

RUTH: You're bankrupt already.

JACK: That's because I was married once.

RUTH: No, that's because you think you can live on six thousand dollars a year.

JACK: So call me an idealist.

RUTH: Freeloader.

JACK: Capitalist.

RUTH: Not all marriages have to be as bad as yours was, you know.

JACK: It's all I have to go on.

RUTH: Joan wasn't *every* wife.

JACK: Right.

RUTH: We've just started off so well, Jack!

JACK: But we have scarcely begun to taste our joys! Six months?

RUTH: Six months is a lot of time to get to know a person.

JACK: Hardly the "t" in "tick" on eternity's clock.

RUTH: I'm not saying *tomorrow*. I'm not saying we have to run off and hire the first J.P. we come to.

JACK: Jewish J.P.

RUTH: Well that goes without saying.

JACK: We're still young anyway. Who needs a J.P., Jewish or otherwise?

RUTH: We're not twenty-five anymore, Jack.

JACK: What? We're *not*?

JACK AND RUTH: *Uh-oh!*

RUTH: Not only that, but we won't get to play moony-eyed lovers in bed forever.

JACK: If we got married we wouldn't get to do *anything* in bed together.

RUTH: Now watch yourself.

JACK: I speak from personal experience.

RUTH: But that was in another century. And besides, the bitch was bored by sex.

JACK: Everybody's bored by sex in marriage. Except adulterers. It's a rule of nature. Even *I* was bored by sex in marriage.

The moment you say "I do," your sex glands pack up and head into retirement, and the perfumes that the body gives off for mutual attraction turn to vinegar. That person you used to spend whole weekends with, linked at the groin—? You start staying up a little later so they'll go to bed before you and you won't have to endure having sex with them. Your husband's cock starts to look about as attractive as an old carrot, and your wife's nipples start to look about as kissable as ink erasers. Suddenly you notice little hairs sprouting from your partner's ears. . . .

RUTH: Don't you ever stop?

JACK: No. Wake up alongside the same *body* every morning? *Yech!*

RUTH: Thank you!

JACK: Anyway, you'd have to get your parents to talk to me first.

RUTH: All right, all right . . .

JACK: Rather a major undertaking.

RUTH: Can we—?

JACK: Just because my name doesn't end in -berg, -stein, or -erkowitz, they won't enter a room with me without hanging garlic around their necks first. I can't believe they actually agreed to come over tonight.

RUTH: My parents aren't the question.

JACK: What, even though they think I'm polluting their daughter with my goyish sperm? Even though your mother boiled her hand after the last time I shook it? Even though they threatened to write you out of their goddamn *will* if you marry someone who isn't Jewish?

RUTH: All right.

JACK: Christ. *Religion.*

RUTH: I know—

JACK AND RUTH: *Superstition and slavery.*

JACK: Well that's all religion is. Superstition and slavery.

RUTH: Yes I think I've heard this speech someplace before.

JACK: What century are we in, anyway?

RUTH: Can we stop? Please?

(*Small pause.*)

JACK: Was somebody just curmudging in here—?

RUTH: Yes, dear. *You.*

JACK: Oh Christ, I'm sorry, sheriff. I don't know what came over me.

RUTH: Just the usual.

JACK: But you know that it isn't anything personal, against any one religion.

RUTH: I know.

JACK: I mean, you know that my secret ambition is to assassinate the Pope. First I'll anesthetize him with a lot of cannoli, then *BLAM!*—the water pistol. "I'm melting! All my beautiful evil!" However you say that in Latin.

RUTH: Oh you Catholics, boy. You are really something.

JACK: Excuse me, but I am *not* a Catholic.

RUTH: Okay, lapsed Catholic.

JACK: Ex-lapsed. I just happened to be born into a Catholic family.

RUTH: It's the same thing.

JACK: Everybody who isn't Catholic thinks that. Especially Jews, who can't be lapsed even if they want to be.

RUTH: You might *think* you shake it, but you never *really* shake it.

JACK: I always shake it. Otherwise you get pee all over your shorts.

RUTH: How come everybody I know who was brought up Catholic acts like all religions are an insult to their integrity?

JACK: An insult to my integrity! A perfect description, thank you.

RUTH: Like they got jilted by God, or something. . . .

JACK: Haven't your parents caught on that none of your boyfriends for the last fifteen years have been Jewish? Haven't they cottoned to the fact that Semitic lips have not touched yours since that guy at college who later had a sex-change operation?

RUTH: They caught on, all right. That's what they're worried about.

JACK: My parents don't mind that you're Jewish.

RUTH: Yes they do.

JACK: No they don't.

RUTH: I give your parents a first-class case of the Hebrew-jebrews.

JACK: They've never said a single thing about you being Jewish!

RUTH: Maybe they don't say anything outwardly. But inwardly they mind very *much* that I'm Jewish. That Dolby silence at the table when any reference to my being Jewish came up?

JACK: There are a lot of silences at my parents' table about a lot of things. That's what goyish means. "Silent at table."

RUTH: That killing politeness?

JACK: Oh, it's their *politeness* that persecuted you. Isn't that better than your parents—who inwardly mind that I'm not Jewish and outwardly say it all the time?

RUTH: At least they don't hide their convictions behind a slitty-eyed grin.

JACK: Ah. Convictions. Another fine word for bigotry.

RUTH: What, your parents don't have "convictions"?

JACK: My parents' convictions at least leave room for different "convictions" at the table.

RUTH: I thought that you despised your parents' convictions.

JACK: Well I do, mostly, but I'm making a convenient exception.

RUTH: Everybody does.

JACK: Maybe if your parents wore glasses with little dark wigs and big noses painted on the lenses they could look at me and see me as one of their own kind.

RUTH: No racial stereotypes, please.

JACK: Oh right. This from the girl who planned the How-to-Be-Jewish kit.

RUTH: Okay . . .

JACK: The ads at the back of the *New Yorker*? "You too can say 'Nu' in five languages"—?

RUTH: That was in a moment of drunken abandon.

JACK: Oh that excuses it.

RUTH: Anyway did I say that or did you say that?

JACK: You said that.

RUTH: Well I can say those things. You can't.

(*Lights suddenly change to glaringly bright.*)

JACK (*sudden furious heat*): Yeah? What makes it all right in your mouth and sacrilege in mine? How come you can insult the Germans and the French, but your own tribe is sacred?

(*The phone rings. The lights change back. Calmer rhythm again.*)

RUTH: Parents, parents, everything's parents. Who invented parents, anyway?

JACK: J. Robert Oppenheimer. I just never think about them.

RUTH: I know.

JACK: Parents? Feh! World's biggest waste of time. I mean, what century are we in, anyway? (*He notices that she's looking at him intently.*) What. What's this gimlet-eyed look?

RUTH: Nothing. Just tell me I'm beautiful.

JACK: You're *extremely* beautiful. For your age.

RUTH: You dog!

JACK: You're very well preserved.

RUTH: You hound! You beast!

JACK: A little crow's-foot here and there . . .

RUTH: You cad! (*Sudden swoon.*) Oh Nicky . . .

JACK: Oh Nora . . . (*They swoon into bed together and embrace, just as the alarm clock goes off.*)

RUTH: Christ, it's six o'clock! We have to get dressed! (*She turns off the alarm and runs into the bathroom.* JACK *stares at the place on the bed where she had been, as if she's just disappeared.*)

JACK: Nora? *Nora . . . ?* OH GOD, NORA!!!

RUTH (*from the bathroom*): Six o'clock, pal!

JACK: Plenty of time, plenty of time . . . Everybody's going to be fashionably late anyway. (RUTH *appears in the bathroom doorway with a toothbrush.*)

RUTH: Rise 'n' shine, lover.

JACK: 'Tis true 'tis day—what though it be?
Oh wilt thou therefore rise from me?
Why should we rise because 'tis light?
Did we lie down because 'twas night?

RUTH (*completes the poem*): Burma Shave. Do you want to wash up in here? Scrape off some of the funk?

JACK (*starts to dress*): No, I want to reek of sex. I want everybody exchanging furtive glances across the room and wondering why the place smells like an aquarium.

RUTH (*in bathroom*): Like a what?

JACK: An aquarium.

RUTH (*puts her head into the room*): If you tell that joke tonight, I'll kill you.

JACK: Who, me?

RUTH: Yeah, you.

JACK: Would it be all over?

RUTH: It would *definitely* be all over.

JACK: Seems to take so little these days. Where are the fifty-year attachments of yesteryear? The golden anniversaries. The silver-haired couples taking their third honeymoon in the Poconos. Lost to the weekend liaison and the one-night stand.

RUTH: Lost to the search for the liaison d'être.

JACK: Ouch, ouch, ouch.

RUTH: Sorry. Couldn't help it.

JACK: One more of those and you're out, kid.

RUTH: You don't know how long I've been saving that one up.

JACK: Hey what've you got playing on your inner radio?

RUTH: Bizet. *Pearl Fishers.*

JACK: Ah! *Les Pêcheurs de perles!* I've had Joan Armatrading going for about three days, and she is driving me crazy. Right . . . here. (*Taps the center of his forehead. Sings from "Takin' My Baby Uptown."*)

> What we've got is the past
> What we've got is the past
> What we've got is the past—

RUTH: The best.

JACK: Huh?

RUTH: That line is, "What we've got is the *best.*"

JACK: "What we've got is the past."

RUTH: Best.

JACK: Past.

RUTH: Best.

JACK: Oh good. Let's have a fight.

RUTH: We never fight. Do you realize that?

JACK: We disagree. We disagree all the time.

RUTH: But we've never had a real knock-down-drag-out brawl.

JACK: We can practice up for when we need it. Anyway, give me a few bars of Bizet and drive the bitch off my inner radio, will you?

RUTH (*sings*): *"Au fond du temple saint."*

RUTH AND JACK: *"Paré de fleurs et d'or."*

RUTH: *"Une femme apparait."*

JACK: *"Une femme apparait."*

RUTH AND JACK: *"Je crois la voir encore!"* (RUTH *stops singing, but* JACK *goes on, standing on the bed to vocalize dramatically.*)

JACK: *"C'est elle! C'est la desse! Plus charmante et plus belle!"* (*Stops.*) What's the matter? I'm pearl-fishing all by myself here suddenly.

RUTH: I had a thought the other day.

JACK: Think it for me.

RUTH: Do you remember how somebody once said that hell is other people?

JACK: Yeah. Sartre the Fartre.

RUTH: Hell isn't other people. Hell is *remembering* other people.

JACK: I don't think I quite follow you, Senator.

RUTH: I mean getting them stuck in your memory. Having to remember certain conversations over and over again. The scenes that keep coming back. Running them over and over again like some broken record . . .

JACK: There's always the bright side of that. The "Ode on a Grecian Urn" side.

RUTH: Which is—?

JACK: That frozen moment in time. "Forever wilt thou love and she be fair. . . . Forever wilt thou love and she be fair. . . . Forever . . . Forever . . . Forever . . ."

(*The phone rings, and the lights change again to sudden glaring brightness. Immediate change of tone.*)

RUTH: All right, then, leave!

JACK: Fuck you!

RUTH: Leave!

JACK: Fuck you!

RUTH: Then leave!

JACK: Fucking Jap!

RUTH: Will you leave?

JACK: Fucking Princess! Look how *you* turned out!

RUTH: How did I turn out?

JACK: Did you ever think that this isn't even the real issue?

RUTH: It doesn't have anything to do with *believing*.

JACK: Then what does it have to do with?

RUTH: It doesn't have anything to do with believing.

JACK: So what does it have to do with?

RUTH: And what's the *real* issue? Do you want to tell me that?

(*The phone rings, and they go completely still. Lights change back to where they were before. Calm tone again.*)

RUTH: Hell isn't other people. Hell is remembering other people. . . .

JACK: *I* had a thought the other day. About parents.

RUTH: A plan to exterminate them?

JACK: Something like that.

RUTH: How did I ever guess.

JACK: You see in *my* utopia—

RUTH: Yes in *your* utopia—

JACK: In *my* utopia when you turned sixteen you'd get to exchange your parents.

RUTH: Not for other parents.

JACK: Of course not! Who'd want *more parents?*

RUTH: It's a given. (*Realizes.*) *Oops! Joan-phrase!* (*Claps a hand over her mouth.*)

JACK: "It's a *given?*"

RUTH: I'm sorry.

JACK: Boy, did my heart drop out of me!

RUTH: I'm sorry.

JACK: Phew! For a second there I thought I was still married!

RUTH: Relax. Breathe. You're here. You're still single. Still adrift in the world.

JACK: Did you say "adrift"? I'm not adrift.

RUTH: Oh. Sorry. Afloat?

JACK: I'm not afloat either. Maybe ajar. Anyway—*parents.*

RUTH: Oh good. Back to that.

JACK: In my utopia, you'd get to exchange your parents.

RUTH: For—?

JACK: I don't know. What's the exchange rate on parents these days? A coupla glass beads and a chicken pot pie? A ticket to a bingo tournament?

RUTH: Classic Jack . . .

JACK: Anyway they'd be gone. Cashed in. And you wouldn't have to hang out with them—and you wouldn't have to invite them to your birthday parties. They wouldn't even be *allowed* to come to your birthday parties It'd be illegal. They'd be ticketed and towed away.

RUTH: Mmm. Great plan.

JACK: I seem to sense some reservations on your part.

RUTH: Aren't you going to get dressed?

JACK: I *am* dressed. Pants. Shirt. Even socks.

RUTH: I mean dressed.

JACK: Your friends wouldn't recognize me if I wore anything fancier than this. They'd think you dumped me for some worthy capitalist and they'd all come up to me and say, "Did you get a load of that loser she was going out with? Jack something-or-other-that-didn't-end-in-bergstein? Thank God she dumped *that* one, boy."

RUTH: Oh and by the way, Savonarola.

JACK: Uh-oh! I don't like the sound of that at *all*.

RUTH: You be nice to Esther tonight.

JACK: But you know how much I love Esther Trendstein.

RUTH: *Tenn*stein.

JACK: Despite her being a complete maroon.

RUTH: One of these days you're going to slip and really call her that.

JACK: A maroon?

RUTH: I mean it. None of your usual tonight.

JACK: I will be Mister Charm.

RUTH: You said that the last time, when you left the room every time she was in it.

JACK: Do you think she noticed?

RUTH: I think she got the idea.

JACK: Maybe it was the trumpet I used for my exits. What *I* don't understand is how you and that gold-plated Jap ever got to be friends in the first place. (RUTH *says nothing*.) Winner of the Golden Palm de Boredom. (*She still says nothing*.) Did I say something?

RUTH: You know I hate that word.

JACK: Boredom?

RUTH: *Jap*.

JACK: It's the only word that applies.

RUTH: I still hate it.

JACK: The United Nations unanimously declared Esther an international Jewish American Princess. An IJAP.

RUTH: Wouldn't surprise me, coming from the U.N.

JACK: Maybe we shouldn't talk about it.

RUTH: Let's not talk about it.

JACK: Anyway Esther hates me too, so it's mutual.

RUTH: She doesn't hate you.

JACK: She thinks I'm a loser, which is the same thing.

RUTH: But you *are* a loser, darling!

JACK: Oh well that's all right, then.

RUTH: You haven't exactly been a shining financial success up till now, teaching mathematics to fourteen-year-olds for odd change and a school lunch.

JACK: But the lunches are so good.

RUTH: You're not exactly Mister Solvent.

JACK: Who ever said I wanted to be? Who ever said I *should* be?

RUTH: Nothing wrong with a few comforts and a little security.

JACK: I have all the comforts I need, thank you.

RUTH: The complete works of John D. MacDonald and a bottle of Wild Turkey do not comprise a kingly existence.

JACK: With thou beside me in the wilderness they represent a completely fulfilling human life.

RUTH: A bottle of Wild Turkey which *I* bought you, Mister Walden Pond.

JACK: Yeah, send over a refill when you get a chance, will ya?

RUTH: I don't even know how you and John D. MacDonald and the turkey manage to fit into that rathole of an apartment you have.

JACK: Rathole? Rathole?

RUTH: Okay. Parakeet cage.

JACK: Maybe it's a parakeet cage but it's certainly not a rathole. Besides, there's plenty of room over here.

RUTH: Is that what you call comfort?

JACK: In my life there is simplicity, there is integrity, there is unattachment to the things of this world. To Esther Trendstein, the human steam shovel, these things make me about as appealing as the Hunchback of Notre Dame. Unlike the toilet-paper tycoon she married.

RUTH: *Waxed* paper.

JACK: The Jewish Prince Charming. The sheikh of West Ninety-ninth Street. (*Middle Eastern accent.*) "Let me show you my tent. My sheep. My flocks of goats. My beautiful wife. I own her. I have branded my name into her forehead. Someday she will bear me a son. Then I will roast her and eat her."

RUTH: That's not a sheikh. You sound like Dracula.

JACK: "Have I told you that my toilet-paper company earned over four-point-five zillion dollars last year? Now I have bought my fifth Mercedes and the entire state of Montana, for my summer home."

RUTH: What do you want, he's an Israeli.

JACK: Ah-*ha!* Anti-Semitism!

RUTH: I can say that. You can't.

JACK: You know what Esther gave him for Hanukkah?

RUTH: I'm afraid to ask.

JACK: His dick, in a small box.

RUTH: Jack . . .

JACK: My lips are sealed. In wax.

RUTH: You are *impossible*.

JACK: I'm not even probable, but I'm here. Now show me one of your legs. (*She sticks one out.*) I'm young again. Oh God if I had ten lives I'd spend one of them just watching you put on your stockings. I'd just cream my underwear very slowly for threescore and ten years.

RUTH: Is there anything but sex for you?

JACK: Nope. Freud was right. Everything is sex. Except sex, which is money. Which is actually feces. But everything else is sex. The world is ruled by hormones. Estrogen. Endrogen. Nitrogen. Bombay gin.

(*The phone rings.*)

RUTH: Is there anything but sex for you?

JACK: Nope. Freud was right. Everything is sex. Except sex, which is—

(*The phone rings.*)

RUTH: Isn't there anything but sex?

(*The phone rings again.*)

JACK: Anyway, it's not like I haven't had money-making non-loser ideas in my life.

RUTH: Do you mean the punk-rock toothpaste?

JACK: "Deca-Dent"? No, this is different.

RUTH: The bumper stickers? "Have a Nice Bidet"?

JACK: No, this is new. Listen. *Prophylactics for dogs.* (*TV commercial.*) "Love can be a bitch, so give your dog Cockers! Lubricated or regular." Market it right and I could make a million. And Esther would shit in her Hammacher-Schlemmer diapers.

RUTH: What is this mishegaas men always have about their girl-friends' friends?

JACK: Mishegaas? *Moi?*

RUTH: It's so weird. At least you like Bob and Sandy.

JACK: I love Bob and Sandy. But that's because they're tall, thin and funny, like us.

RUTH: You like Morrie and Jean.

JACK: I adore Morrie and Jean.

RUTH: And Harry and Robin.

JACK: I venerate Harry and Robin.

RUTH: I wish we could've had some of *your* friends over.

JACK: I don't have any friends. Not to call up, anyway.

RUTH: It's true, isn't it . . .

JACK: Only to hang up on.

RUTH: Why is that? Why don't you have any friends?

JACK: You're my friend. You and the fourteen-year-olds. (*He notices the shoes she is putting on.*) Good *God!*

RUTH: What.

JACK: What are those?

RUTH: They are called shoes in my language.

JACK: I recognized the general species, but—*blue shoes?*

RUTH: What's wrong with them?

JACK: BLUE SHOES?

RUTH: Yeah. Blue shoes.

JACK: Do you *need* a pair of blue shoes?

RUTH: I got them to go with my dress.

JACK: Oh the socialist police will be on your ass about this one. Karl Marx is going to cream you, down at the station.

RUTH: Hey, it's my birthday, asshole.

JACK: Tell that to the starving children of India.

(*The phone rings.*)

It's the socialist police! Hide, quick!

(*The phone rings again.*)

Go away! We don't want any!

RUTH: Somebody's probably late. Want to get it?

JACK (*picks up the receiver*): Gotham porno line, Pinky speaking.—Hello? (*Listens.*) I know you're there, sir. I can hear you breathing.

RUTH: Give me that.

JACK: It's just me, the goyish boychekel.

RUTH: Jack, give me that. (*Takes the receiver.*) Hi, Dad. Sorry about that. . . . What's up, chronically late again, or—? (*Stops, listens.*) Oh. (*Listens.*) Uh-huh . . . (*Listens.*) No, it's *not* all right, actually. . . . (*Listens.*) Well I hope you're going to change your— (*Listens.*) Okay. Okay. (*Listens.*) No, don't call me later in the week. I said *don't* call me. 'Bye! (*She bangs down the receiver.*)

JACK: What's the matter?

RUTH: They're not coming.

JACK: Oh. Did he bother to make any flimsy excuses?

RUTH: No.

JACK: Did he say *anything?*

RUTH: He said they'd take me out to dinner later in the week.

JACK: Well that was nice of him. Usual understanding, sensitive guy.

(*Silence.*)

RUTH: I'm sorry.

JACK: Don't be sorry.

RUTH: I'm sorry anyway, I feel sorry. God, they are such *assholes*.

JACK: They're parents, what do you expect? And *you* don't have anything to be sorry about.

RUTH: They're my parents. That's all.

JACK: Look. Do you want me to leave so that they can come to your party?

RUTH: What? Don't be crazy.

(*Pause.*)

I don't know what I'm going to tell people when my parents don't show up at the party.

JACK: Tell them the truth. Say that your father's rounding up a posse for me down at B'nai B'rith. (RUTH *says nothing*.) Does anyone expect a woman of your, ah, age to have her parents at her birthday party anyway? It's not like we're bobbing for apples, here. (RUTH *says nothing*.) Well! It's never been *this* bad before. Who says there's no such thing as progress?

RUTH: I could just kill him.

JACK: Oh what the hell. Say antidisestablishmentarianism. (*She says nothing*.) Say "pork bellies." (*She says nothing*.) Say "vagina."

RUTH: Vagina.

JACK: Say it happier.

RUTH: Vagina.

JACK: Say "magic fingers."

RUTH: Magic fingers.

JACK: Say— (*She kisses him*.) Don't say a word. You are cured. Arise, take up thy pallet and go.

RUTH: Oh shut up.

JACK: And behold, he did shut up.

RUTH: You know what I should have said to him? Never mind. It's not important.

JACK: The French have a term for that.

RUTH: For what.

JACK: Stairway thoughts.

RUTH: Stairway thoughts? What's the English for that?

JACK: It's what you think of when you're out on the stairs going down and you realize what you should've said to the bastard back there. Stairway thoughts.

RUTH: Trust the French.

JACK: *Esprit d'escalier.*

RUTH: Don't be pedantic.

JACK: Hey don't blame me, blame the French. They thought of it. (*She says nothing.*) Is everything ready in the kitchen?

RUTH: We just have to put it all out.

JACK: You okay?

RUTH: No.

JACK: Don't let it get you down.

RUTH: Of course it's going to get me down.

JACK: They're just parents. And *I'm* not hurt.

RUTH: Sure.

JACK: Okay, I'm hurt and I hate the bastards and I think we'll have more fun without 'em anyway. And I'll get more food because I won't have to fight your father for the chip dip.

RUTH: I didn't even really want them here, I just invited them to be nice. To be a *good daughter.* Why do I always do that? Don't I ever learn?

JACK: They're just parents. Fuck 'em.

RUTH: Who invented parents, anyway.

JACK: Psychiatrists. But who invented children? Ha! Can you answer me *that* question, Professor? Those beings designed by some wicked deity to scream in your ear, shit in your hand, and bankrupt you? (*She says nothing.*) What. What's this gimlet-eyed look?

RUTH: I want them sometime, you know. Kids, I mean.

JACK: I know.

RUTH: The two of us could make wonderful kids, Pinky.

JACK: We *are* wonderful kids.

RUTH: We could breed a whole crop of tall, thin and funny children. The vanguard in that utopian future when everybody will be tall, thin and funny. And we'd be the ones who started it.

JACK: What would you do if they ended up short, fat and dull?

RUTH: Stretch 'em, put 'em on a diet, and teach 'em some jokes.

JACK: Well no matter what they turned out to be, if they had any of my blood in them your mother would have them kidnapped and sent to a kibbutz for deprogramming. And bye-bye utopia.

RUTH: You know that's why Bob and Sandy went to Aruba.

JACK: To join a kibbutz?

RUTH: To make a baby.

JACK: Oh.

RUTH: We're not twenty-five years old anymore, Jack.

JACK: So I hear.

(*Pause.*)

JACK: Well listen, you have to be your thin, witty and charming self in about fifteen minutes, so you'd better get it together. People will think we've been having a serious conversation or something.

RUTH: We do have a good time together, don't we.

JACK: Sure. We're friends. It's a new concept in relationships. Friends and lovers simultaneously instead of consecutively. The way things are supposed to be in that world without canned spaghetti or toupées. Remember? So hey. Since we *are* such good friends . . . you wanna fuck, pal?

RUTH: Ohhhhhhhhh no . . . (*She moves away and he pursues.*)

JACK: Come on, just a quickie.

RUTH: Why does this always happen right before a party?

JACK: I won't even take my pants off. We'll do it Polish-style.

RUTH: Get away from me, you fiend!

JACK: All you have to do is lower your panties and we can do it on the floor.

RUTH: We're always late for things because of this.

JACK: One last fuck.

RUTH: Exactly.

JACK: Only we'll make it quick and steamy instead of the usual slow and luscious.

RUTH: You always say that and we're always forty-five minutes late.

JACK: We've never regretted it yet.

RUTH: You have to do something about this chronic horniness.

JACK: It's my tragic flaw. Horniness is next to tardiness. (*Suddenly pointing in the air as a diversionary tactic.*) Look! (*As she looks there, he dives across the bed to catch her, but she jumps back, eluding him.*)

RUTH: Everybody's coming *here* this time. We can't keep them waiting at the door.

JACK: We'll let 'em in and they can watch.

RUTH: Jack . . .

JACK: It'll be the real thing, right in front of their eyes. The zipless fuck. The beatific vision. The second coming. Or third or fourth. So come on, what do you say? Huh? Hm? Huh? Bed? Sex? Bed?

RUTH: Will you ever grow up?

JACK: Nope. Come on. You'll love it. So will I.

RUTH: Do you promise we'll be quick?

JACK: Scout's honor. Ten minutes or under.

RUTH: One foot on the floor at all times?

JACK: And both hands on the ceiling.

RUTH: You're on.

(*They start to undress. The doorbell rings. They stop.*)

JACK: We could still do it really quick.

RUTH: Sorry, pal. Fate has spoken.

JACK: Oh my balls are going to be sapphire blue all night.

RUTH: Good. They'll match my shoes.

JACK: If you see me walking funny, you'll know why.

RUTH: Just keep your legs crossed.

JACK: And it'll be *your fault*. (*Doorbell.*)

RUTH: Just a minute!

JACK: Last chance.

RUTH: Down, Casanova. And remember what I said.

JACK: What did you say?

RUTH: Are you ready to face the world? Balls tucked in?

JACK: You may fire when ready, Grisley.

BLACKOUT

ACT TWO

Just after the party. Streamers and confetti all over the floor.

JACK: Wooooeeee!

RUTH (*jive talk*): Everybody lookin' good! (*They jitterbug a couple of steps.*)

JACK: Great party, Pinkerstein.

RUTH: Oh you think so?

JACK: I do, I do, I do. I definitely do. The bash of the year.

RUTH: Everybody seemed to have an all-right time, all right.

JACK: Oh will you wipe that goddamn false modesty off your beautiful face?

RUTH: Hee hee hee.

JACK: You should've had the *Times* here to review it! This party could've run for months!

RUTH: With a touring company.

JACK: With touring companies playing Peoria, Paris and Bangkok!

RUTH: Now *this* is the way to get old.

JACK: With Lauren Bacall playing you.

RUTH: Hey. Not *that* old.

JACK: Oops.

(*They collapse crosswise on the bed and take breaths.*)

RUTH: Phew.

JACK: Well.

RUTH: Wow.

JACK: Yeah.

RUTH: Decompression chamber, please!

JACK: Nothing like a good party to give you a case of the bends.

RUTH: The aerobic hostess. Only if everybody was having such a good time, what was that loud stampede to get out of here?

JACK: Yeah. It's not even that late.

RUTH: The way everybody headed for the door I thought my apartment had hit an iceberg or something.

JACK: Maybe everybody started worrying you'd ask them to clean up. They sure did a great job of turning your place into a pig sty. Are you sure those were your *friends?*

RUTH: Could be a new brand of terrorist. They drive up in a van and dump garbage all over your floor, then vanish into the night.

JACK: Are we something?

RUTH: We are something. (*Silence.*) What are we?

JACK: Expert party-givers.

RUTH: Oh yeah. Well I guess we might as well start excavating. (*She rises.*)

JACK: Aw, leave it for tomorrow. Come on back down and give your old pal a nuzzle.

RUTH: A nuzzle?

JACK: A nuzzle. The nuzzle is mine. (*She joins him on the bed and he puts his arms around her.*)

RUTH: Nuzzle nuzzle nuzzle.

JACK: And may I say—you looked fabulous.

RUTH: For my age. I know.

JACK: I can't speak for anyone else, but I spent the entire evening in a state of sexual arousal, just looking at you. Maybe it was the expensive blue shoes.

RUTH: Oh I'll never hear the end of them, will I.

JACK: I wanted to make violent passionate love with you right on the floor, but then I saw that Esther had covered it with tortilla chips. No doubt part of a conscious plot to keep us apart.

RUTH: By the way.

JACK: Yes?

RUTH: You were terrific. Thanks.

JACK: Oh. You were terrific too. (*Small pause.*) What were we terrific for?

RUTH: I mean with Esther.

JACK (*as if trying to remember*): Esther, Esther . . .

RUTH: I couldn't believe how nice you were being to her. I mean, actually standing in conversation with her—?

JACK: It wasn't that hard. I was wearing earplugs.

RUTH: I mean it, Jack.

JACK: Well *she started it*. She sure was in a bouncy mood tonight.

RUTH: Mm.

JACK: Disgustingly bouncy. And the sheikh seemed absolutely ecstatic. As usual, I got treated to the *Reader's Digest* condensed version of the *Joys of Yiddish*. (*Accent.*) "And this shmeggege was ganz meshuggeneh, so I took his mezzuzah and I hit him on the kopf."

RUTH: I'm going to get out of these clothes.

JACK: Now you're talking. Just let me get my binoculars. (*She starts to undress. He puts his hands to his eyes like binoculars.*)

The aerobic hostess disrobes. (*He watches for a moment.*) Sandy looked good tonight.

RUTH: She did look pretty good.

JACK: Was the trip to Aruba successful? Is she with child?

(*Small pause.*)

RUTH: They don't know yet.

JACK: Jean looked good.

RUTH: Jean looked *very* good. Did she turn you on?

JACK: A leetle, yes.

RUTH: But of course.

JACK: In that dress? Whoo! *Quelle clivage!*

RUTH: Did you know they're buying a house?

JACK: Huh.

RUTH: Upstate.

JACK: Upscale upstate. *Per aspera ad . . .* upstate. (RUTH *stops dressing and stands very still.*) What.

RUTH: Nothing. Just got tired, all of a sudden.

JACK: Elizabeth looked good.

RUTH: Elizabeth? Elizabeth looked *awful.*

JACK: You're right. She did look pretty awful.

RUTH: All pasty-faced and wrinkled.

JACK: Well that's what comes of having the sex life of a door-knob.

RUTH: That's what comes of living by yourself for ten years.

JACK: Same thing.

RUTH: Isn't there anything but sex for you?

JACK: Yes, there are also anchovies. And dancing. Outside of those things lies the void.

RUTH: There was little enough dancing, tonight. For what was supposed to be a good party. How come nobody was out on the floor but us?

JACK: Mm. Especially with Joan Armatrading singing her heart out. (*Sings.*)

> What we've got is the best
> What we've got is the best
> What we've got—

RUTH: The past.

JACK: Huh?

RUTH: That line is, "What we've got is the *past.*"

JACK: Best.

RUTH: Past.

JACK: Best.

RUTH: Past.

JACK: Oh good, let's have a fight. Liven things up a little.

RUTH: Do you realize that we've never had a fight? I mean a real knock-down-drag-out brawl?

JACK: I leave those to your married friends.

RUTH: We never shout, or throw things. . . . What the hell's wrong with us?

JACK: We're not made to fight, we're made to love. We are made . . . to *love.*

RUTH: Excuse me, Cupid. You don't believe in love. Remember?

JACK: What? I *don't?*

RUTH AND JACK: *Uh-oh!*

JACK: You are so Schlegel. I can't say anything without you catching me right out.

RUTH: Have you ever thought that you should be going out with Elizabeth?

JACK: Me? *What?* Go out with Elizabeth?

RUTH: Yeah. Or somebody *like* Elizabeth?

JACK: You just finished telling me she's all pasty-faced and wrinkled. What the hell are you fobbing her off on *me* for?

RUTH: Just a thought.

JACK: Gadzooks! (*He starts to change back into his robe.*)

RUTH: Well she's goyish, and you're goyish, so . . .

JACK: So you thought we could buy a white clapboard house in Connecticut and *goy* together. Is that the idea?

RUTH: Just a thought.

JACK: Is that your two-dimensional stereotypical vision? And I'm going out with *you.* Remember?

RUTH: Oh yeah. *Duhh.*

JACK: *Duhh.*

(*The phone rings. The lights change, and they are still.*)

RUTH: Where does this fragility come from? Like people are made out of glass now . . . Are we really looser and more flexible than our great-great-grandparents, or more brittle? Or more cowardly. My grandparents were married for seventy-three years! Is that just a thing of the past now, like buggy whips and the minuct? Where are the fifty-year attachments of yesteryear? The silver-haired couples taking their third honeymoon in the Poconos? Is all that gone now?

(*The phone rings and they are in motion again.*)

JACK: Hey what was all that crap about temple tonight? What was all that between you and Esther?

RUTH: She wants me to come to her temple for Rosh Hashanah.

JACK: Why?

RUTH: What do you mean, why.

JACK: You're not going to go, are you?

RUTH: Uh-huh.

JACK: To Rosh Hashanah services?

RUTH: Of course I'm going to go.

JACK: But what for? When was the last time you went to Rosh Hashanah services?

RUTH: I happen to go to Rosh Hashanah services every year.

JACK: Oh.

RUTH: It's not a felony, you know. It's Rosh Hashanah services.

JACK: But you don't believe all that stuff.

RUTH: It doesn't have anything to do with believing.

JACK: So what does it have to do with?

RUTH: It doesn't have anything to do with believing.

JACK: So what does it have to do with?

RUTH: It doesn't have anything to do with believing.

JACK: Superstition and slavery, in equal parts. This month Rosh Hashanah services, next month the ritual baths to purify your uncleanness. Then, what, you'll shave your head and start saying all those prayers thanking God you're not a woman?

RUTH: You don't know what you're talking about, buddy.

JACK: Okay. I don't know what I'm talking about.

RUTH: And you're more than welcome to come along too.

JACK: Oh sure. I can see that.

RUTH: I *am* a Jew, you know.

JACK: A Jew? No. Maybe Jew . . . *ish,* but not a Jew. You're Pinky.

(*The phone rings. They pay no attention.*)

RUTH: Did anybody call tonight?

JACK: No. Not that I know of. Not that I heard. Why.

RUTH: Nothing.

JACK: Do you think you won the lottery?

RUTH: Do you know that he didn't even wish me a happy birthday?

JACK: Who?

RUTH: When he called?— My father.

JACK: Oh. (*Small pause.*) Well maybe we didn't hear the phone with all the racket.

RUTH: I know it's stupid.

JACK: It's not stupid.

RUTH: Stupid stuff . . . You know what I should've said to him? Forget it. It's not important.

JACK: The French have a term for that, you know.

RUTH: Do you know that he didn't even wish me a happy birthday? (JACK *comes up behind her and kisses the back of her neck.*)

JACK: Happy birthday, babe. I'll make up the difference. (*Kisses her neck again. She turns and looks at him hard.*) What. What's this look.

RUTH: Nothing.

JACK: Forgot what I looked like again, huh. (*They are still. Then in motion again.*) Hey, who's this guy Josh who was here tonight?

RUTH: Josh?

JACK: Yeah. *Josh.*

RUTH: He's an old friend.

JACK: You seemed very surprised to see him, for an old friend.

RUTH: I didn't expect him to be here.

JACK: But you don't have any fat friends. None that you've confessed to, anyway.

RUTH: He's a doctor.

JACK: Is that a non sequitur? Or an explanation for him being fat? (*She says nothing.*) Is this that platonic guy you were going out with, or . . . ?

RUTH: No, it's not him.

JACK: Well whoever he is, he certainly seemed interested in my living arrangements. Kept asking me if I *lived* here. I wondered if he wanted to take out an option on the lease or something. (*She says nothing.*) So?

RUTH: So what.

JACK: So who is this mystery guest?

RUTH: Esther and I met him at her cousin's anniversary thing.

JACK: What, a couple of months ago? That's not exactly what I'd call an old friend.

RUTH: I think she knew him from before, somehow.

JACK: Uh-huh. And—let me guess. You met him at Esther's cousin's anniversary thing, and he asked you out. (RUTH *says nothing*.) Did he ask you out?

RUTH: He did, actually.

JACK: So what did you do?

RUTH: I said I was going out with somebody else.

JACK: And?

RUTH: And what?

JACK: You tell him you're going out with somebody else so he shows up at your birthday party?

RUTH: He's been calling me up every now and again.

JACK: Oh.

RUTH: Look. I didn't expect him to be here tonight. Esther brought him.

JACK: What for?

RUTH: I don't know.

JACK: Did you ever go out with him?

RUTH: No!

JACK: Just asking. Just asking.

RUTH: There's no need to be jealous or anything.

JACK: I'm not jealous.

RUTH: He'd call me up every once in a while to talk. That's all.

JACK: Okay.

RUTH: At the office.

JACK: Okay.

RUTH: I didn't call *him*.

JACK: Okay.

(*They undress in silence for a moment.*)

RUTH: Are you upset?

JACK: No.

RUTH: So what are you?

JACK: I'm not surprised, anyway. Everybody I've ever gone out with has done that.

RUTH: Done what.

JACK: Kept somebody in reserve. Kept somebody around for just-in-case-things-don't-work-out.

RUTH (*overlapping his final words*): I wasn't keeping him in reserve, Jack!

JACK: Oh come on, Ruth.

RUTH: I wasn't!

JACK: Come on. Everybody does it. Keeps somebody around for just-in-case-you-happen-to-break-up.

RUTH: He's nothing. He's nobody.

JACK: It's fine. Really. I'm sorry I asked. I'm sorry I butted in.

RUTH: You didn't butt in on anything.

JACK: This was just a different way of finding out about it. Usually there's an inopportune phone call one night when you pick up instead of her, and you find out that she and some guy have been "just talking on the phone," quote unquote, every week. It's modern life. It's nothing. Big deal.

RUTH: Have *you* been keeping somebody in reserve?

JACK: I just wish I hadn't been so fucking nice to Esther tonight. I should've known that any slight advance in civility is just compensation for some sleazeball activity under the table.

RUTH: Oh Christ . . .

JACK: No wonder she was in such a bouncy mood tonight. She was matchmaking! Too bad your parents weren't here. Your old man probably would've paid this guy cold hard cash to take you off my hands. Nice fat doctor like that, correct genetic composition and everything.

RUTH: The reason that Esther was in such a "bouncy mood" tonight is that she thinks she's pregnant.

JACK: Oh.

RUTH: *That's* why. The only reason they didn't tell everybody is that they're not absolutely sure.

(*Pause.*)

JACK: Well great. I'm sure the sheikh must be delighted. He'll probably—

RUTH: Don't make any cracks, Jack. Please.

JACK: What did you say to her?

RUTH: I said I was happy for her.

JACK: Are you?

RUTH: Yes.

JACK: Seems motherhood is very in.

RUTH: Motherhood is in. Marriage is in.

JACK: What *century* are we in? Oh for that utopian future when marriage is dusty antique!

RUTH: When women will still be doing the dusting, no doubt.

JACK: But you know Esther isn't going to have just *one* kid. Uh-uh. Any shmo can have one kid—so Esther's going to have five, all at once. It's a bigger return on her investment. Sleeping with the sheikh, I mean. It's more for her to show off at Zabar's. Joshua, Matthew, Scott, Max and Elijah. And you know what she's going to give birth to, don't you? If she has quintuplets? (RUTH *says nothing*.) You know what Esther's going to give birth to?

RUTH (*reluctantly*): What.

JACK: *Poly*-esters. Ha, ha, ha, ha, ha. Is this a clever child?

RUTH: It's a clever child.

JACK: Am I a clever little boy?

RUTH: I want them sometime too, Jack. I want kids sometime.

JACK: I know that.

RUTH: And the two of us could make wonderful kids, Pinky.

JACK: We *are* wonderful kids.

RUTH: A whole crop of tall, thin and funny children.

JACK: What'll you do if they end up short, fat and dull?

RUTH: It's not like we're twenty-five anymore, Jack.

JACK: You're repeating yourself. (*Silence*.) But hey! Did I tell you my new moneymaking idea? This is going to make me richer than the sheikh. Listen to this: *braille pajamas*. What do you think? This is for all those nights when you wake up in terror and you don't know where you are. You sit up in the dark and you clutch your heart and you say, "Oh my God, where am I?!" Well with my pajamas, the name of the place you're in is pasted over the pocket in braille, so you'd go, "Oh my God, where am—" (*Stops. Clutches his heart. Feels the "patch" and calms down*.) "Oh. I'm in Singapore." Or Philadelphia, or wherever you happen to be. You're not impressed, I can tell. But think of the million-and-one other uses. Like when you wake up in the dark and you can't remember who you're sleeping with. "Oh my God, who is this?!" (*Clutches his heart, he feels the "patch" and calms down.*) Oh. It's Ruth. Phew! Of course everybody'd have to learn braille. But think how that would promote understanding between the seeing-impaired and the sought. So what do you think?

RUTH: Jack, will you marry me? (*Silence.*)

JACK: I beg your pardon?

RUTH: Will you marry me, Jack? (*Another silence.*)

JACK: Don't kid around.

RUTH: I'm not kidding around.

JACK: *Marry* you? As in—?

RUTH: As in marriage, yes. That ancient ruse to start a home—? Still popular in certain parts of the world, you know.

JACK: You don't want to get married, Ruth.

RUTH: Let me try this again. Jack, will you marry me?

JACK: This is kinda sudden, Doc.

RUTH: Not really.

JACK: So what does this mean, that I have to tell you right *now?*

RUTH: I guess that's what it does mean.

JACK: Tonight? This minute?

RUTH: It's not like you haven't had time. It's not like you haven't had time to think about this.

JACK: I wasn't thinking about it.

RUTH: *I* was thinking about it.

JACK: Six months isn't all that much time, Ruth.

RUTH: At our age it's a lot of time.

JACK: "At our age"? What does that mean? Six months isn't even long enough for me to find out that you go to Rosh Hashanah services every year! Just think what we could find out in the *next* six months.

RUTH: I don't have six more months to wait for you.

JACK: You haven't been waiting for me. I've been right here! I was at the party, remember? The guy you danced with? With the hard-on?

RUTH: Will you marry me, Jack?

JACK: Okay. Well. What about your parents, what are they—

RUTH (*over his last words*): Forget about my parents.

JACK: But they'd never let you—

RUTH: *Forget* about my parents. This is about us.

JACK: Come on, Ruth. You know what this is.

RUTH: No. What is this?

JACK: You have all your friends over, you see that most of them are married, and you want to be like all your friends. This isn't even you talking!

RUTH: Yes it is me talking.

JACK: This is Esther talking! Don't you see the connection to what she told you tonight? Esther has a baby so *you* have to have a baby. This isn't about marriage, or motherhood. This is about keeping up with the sheikhs!

RUTH: I want a *husband,* Jack.

JACK: Why?

RUTH: Because I want a husband.

JACK: How traditional.

RUTH: Yes it is traditional. *I'm* traditional.

JACK: No you're not, you're—

RUTH: Yes. I am. And you should know that about me by now. I'm very traditional.

JACK: But you're in the avant-garde of humanity! You're part of the perfect breed of the future!

RUTH: Somehow I don't think I am.

JACK: Tall and thin and funny—?

RUTH: Jack, you ought to be *glad* I'm playing Sadie Hawkins and asking you to marry me. I help you out. I diaper you when you need it. I give you a place to hang around in that isn't a rathole. Excuse me, a parakeet cage. I get you out into the world. I provide you with a circle of friends which you otherwise don't have. It's a real life, Jack. It's adult life.

JACK: Would marriage help me keep my hair?

RUTH: Yes. And it'd give you somebody to curmudge with when you're eighty.

JACK: Can I still be thirteen when I'm eighty?

RUTH: No. But you'll have someone to be with. Okay, yes, maybe sex will be nasty, poor, brutish, and short.

JACK: When there *is* any.

RUTH: When there is any. But sex is not all there is to life.

JACK: Well . . . it's partly all there is.

RUTH: Isn't a body beside you in bed all night, sex or no sex, better than no body at all? You can't go from girlfriend to girlfriend forever. Because after a while you're not going to be boyfriend material anymore. You're going to be a dog's dinner, my son.

JACK: Thank you for that, sweetie.

RUTH: And you could have kids to live with you and visit you and not mind too much that you're a dog's dinner.

JACK: Not if I was *my* kid. If I was *my* kid I wouldn't visit me.

RUTH: Marriage would also lift you up.

JACK: Out of what?

RUTH: To the level you belong on. How long are you going to play math teacher at some backwater school?

JACK: I like paddling around that backwater.

RUTH: But you have so many possibilities. You know so much. You could be something wonderful.

JACK: I thought I was something wonderful. A math teacher.

RUTH: Right now you're just a cog of the cognoscenti.

JACK: Well, maybe. But *I* put the ram in the ram-a-dam-a-ding-dong.

RUTH: I don't want to get old, Jack.

JACK: There's nothing you can do about that.

RUTH: I don't want to get old all by myself. And I don't want to end up like Elizabeth, getting ugly from loneliness.

JACK: But you can get married and still end up old and alone.

RUTH: Yes you can walk into the street and get hit by a truck, too. You have to plan *something*, for Christ's sake, otherwise you're just . . . You have to plan *some* things.

JACK: You're right. What's for breakfast?

RUTH: Can you get serious for just one minute?

JACK: But I've been married, Ruth.

RUTH: Yes I know you've been married.

JACK: You don't even *know* about marriage.

RUTH: I know what I *want* from a marriage.

JACK: You don't know what you're chasing after!

RUTH: I'm chasing after *you!* Against all reason. Against all the laws of physics. Because we fit so well together, and we have such a good time together.

JACK: Isn't that what people are *supposed* to have together?

RUTH: Having fun isn't a marriage.

JACK: Well that's for fucking sure. . . .

RUTH: Being married to Joan wasn't like *all* marriages.

JACK: It was a very good example.

RUTH: People don't *have* to be unhappily married.

JACK: What? They *don't?*

RUTH (*doesn't pick up the routine*): No. They don't.

(*Pause.*)

JACK: Look, can I tell you one story about my marriage? Joan and I once went on vacation and we—

RUTH: But that was years ago, Jack!

JACK: No, listen to this. We were stopping at a motel in—

RUTH: All that stuff is ancient history by now! You're a different person!

JACK: If I'm a different person, then why does that still hurt? Why is it still burned in?

RUTH: Because you *let* it hurt you.

JACK: No.

RUTH: It's *old,* Jack.

JACK: Not to me, it's not. As far as I'm concerned, that shit all happened this morning.

RUTH: Okay, it happened this morning. Are you going to let it spoil the rest of your day? Can't you just forget about all previous marriages for a minute and think about us and how happy we could be together?

JACK: We *are* happy together.

RUTH: Right!

JACK: So why put a ring on it?

RUTH: If the two of us can't make a marriage work, who can?

JACK: What you're talking about is companionship. And if that's what's important to you, you can get that without being married.

RUTH: Kids are important, too.

JACK: A friend that you can joke around with.

RUTH: Kids are very important.

JACK: Sure, except when they shit in your hand.

RUTH: *Even* when they shit in your hand. *Especially* when they shit in your hand. *You* teach kids. You *love* your kids! You always say the fourteen-year-olds are your friends.

JACK: Yeah, but I don't have to diaper them and have them spit on my shoulder at four in the morning. And do you really want that? You like your sleep as much as I do.

RUTH: Jack . . .

JACK: Who needs a kid anyway? I'm a child at heart.

RUTH: You're a child, all right.

JACK: Only I don't spit on your shoulder at four in the morning. Well, *sometimes* I do, but—

RUTH: That's why this is such a great offer!

JACK: Because I spit on your shoulder?

RUTH: Because you need somebody.

JACK: Yes. *You.* But not *married*-you. You as you are.

RUTH: Why? Why? Why? Why am I different now from what I'd be if I married you?

JACK: Because you'd change.

RUTH: *Ogh!*

JACK: *I'd* change. We'd both change.

RUTH: These stupid ideas about marriage . . .

JACK: We wouldn't take the time anymore. We'd take each other for granted, like all married people do. We'd settle in, and be crushed by gravity. We'd turn from Nick and Nora into Dick and Pat Nixon.

RUTH: This Pavlov reaction about marriage.

JACK: Yes! It's a Pavlov reaction! I admit it! And I'm sorry that I have it. But I have it for a very good reason. Because I have been there, and I have seen it, and it is a horror.

(*Pause.*)

RUTH: I won't live with you if you won't marry me.

JACK: Ruth, do you know any couple as good as we are?

RUTH: Jack, will you marry me?

JACK: No. Wait. Listen. Do you know any two people who get along as well as we do, minute by minute and inch by inch? Who can hum the Mendelssohn Octet *and* quote the entire text of *Animal Crackers*? Let us live together and be funny! And hum!

RUTH: Not on six thousand dollars a year we can't hum together.

JACK: Well—my six thousand plus your six hundred thousand . . .

RUTH: Married or un-married, we can't. Not on six thousand dollars a year.

JACK: I *do* make more than six thousand doll—

RUTH: Whatever you make.

(*Pause.*)

JACK: Do we have to talk about this now? Couldn't we wait for . . .

RUTH: Wait for what.

JACK: Wait until . . .

RUTH: Wait until what.

JACK: *Wait Until Dark.* Audrey Hepburn and Alan Arkin, 1967. Do I roll again?

RUTH: I guess I have my answer.

JACK: No, Ruth—

RUTH: I have my answer. The same answer I've had for six months.

JACK: Yeah. *Happiness.* You—me—together—not married. Somehow those conditions have made us happier than Ivory Soap percentages of the rest of the mortals in this world. And I hate to break it to you, but this is what you do well, my dear Nora. This is what you were made for.

RUTH: I beg your pardon?

JACK: Don't you realize that evolution has made you witty for a reason? It's the next step up the Darwinian ladder from those poor souls who have to bear children! I'm talking biological fact, here! You didn't see this in the *Times*? Funny people are physically unsuited to bearing and raising healthy children because they laugh too much. You get the joke gene, or you get the child gene, it's one or the other.

RUTH: I don't want to joke about this, Jack.

JACK: You're laughing now.

RUTH: I'm not laughing.

JACK: You're stifling a chuckle but I can hear it because your Maxipad is rattling. You zee, *mein Kind,* your agenda and Nature's agenda for you are different. You are suffering from . . . agenda confusion.

RUTH: Can you stop?

JACK: Marriage and children? A definite health hazard for you. And we'd both be lousy parents anyway, let's face it. We'd be horrible at the job!

RUTH: I don't believe that.

JACK: You'd be a terrible mother!

RUTH: I don't believe you just said that. Do you realize what a lousy thing that is to say to somebody?

JACK: I still believe it—

RUTH: I don't care if you believe it!

JACK: All right. I'm sorry I said it.

RUTH: Jack, sometimes you're so— (*The phone rings.*)

Oh *shit.*

JACK: Ruth, we are as— (*The phone rings again.*) We are as good as we are because we are *free.* (*The phone rings.*)

RUTH: Shit . . . (*It rings again.*)

JACK: Should I answer it? (*They wait. It rings again.*) Who could be calling you at one in the morning? (*It rings again. Exasperated,* RUTH *picks up.*)

RUTH: Hello? . . . What? . . . No, we didn't! (*Bangs down the receiver.*)

JACK: What was that?

RUTH: Wanted to know if we'd ordered a pizza. Christ . . .

JACK: Was it pepperoni? If it was pepperoni you should've taken it.

RUTH : Marry me, Jack.

JACK: You don't know what you're asking for.

RUTH: I want a husband. It's that simple.

JACK: But *why?*

RUTH: I can't explain it. It's a given.

JACK: It's a what?

RUTH: It's a given and I'm sorry but I can't avoid saying and doing everything your wife did. You made a mistake in getting married at age seven. Admit it and move on. The world isn't going to stop for you.

(*Pause.*)

JACK: One small problem here is that you want a husband but you don't seem to care who fills the position. You even invited a spare possibility to your party in case I didn't work out.

RUTH: I didn't invite him.

JACK: Before you'd even put the question to me.

RUTH: I didn't invite him.

JACK: Is he outside right now? We can call him in here and you can pop the question to *him*. See if *Josh* works out.

RUTH: *I didn't invite him.* (*Small pause.*) So will you marry me, Jack?

JACK: You don't even know about marriage.

RUTH: I know what I *want* from a marriage.

JACK: At least I admit that I don't like marriage. At least I come out and say it. Do you realize that you've spent fifteen years steering clear of it, very successfully? And talking out of the other side of your mouth? Do you think that it's some kind of *accident* that you're not married now, with kids? Do you think that that is happenstance, Ruth?

RUTH: I've never met the man I wanted to marry, before.

JACK: You haven't been going out with men you *could* marry. I mean men your parents could accept!

RUTH: Forget about my parents. This is about us.

JACK (*overlapping her words slightly*): There are always Jewish men around of all ages—but you haven't been going out with them. You've been going out with men like me. Men you like. Men your parents could never accept.

RUTH: Will you forget about my parents?

JACK (*rising rage*): Do you think that if they didn't come to your birthday party, they'd come to your wedding? To me? No fuckin' way! And you couldn't live with that. Because when it comes down to it, you are a *good daughter*. Because you're thirty-five years old and you still haven't left home and you won't tell your parents to just fuck off!

(*Phone rings. The lights change to a soft glow.*)

Will you marry me, Ruth?

RUTH: What . . . ?

JACK: Will you marry me? You are the exception to every horrible thing that anybody can think about this world. And that I, even *I,* have ever thought about this world. Grass grows in your path where wasteland was before and double rainbows leap into the sky ahead of you. And we will have one hell of a wedding. I'll wear a sweatshirt that says "Superstition and Slavery" and you will go up the aisle in the bluest pair of shoes you ever saw.

(*The phone rings. Lights change back.*)

RUTH: Hell isn't other people. It's remembering other people.

(*The phone rings again.*)

JACK: Okay. So what do we do?

RUTH: Oh Jesus, Jack . . .

JACK: Do I pack up now, or do I get one more night of bliss? Do I at least get a cigarette and a blindfold?

RUTH: Of course you're going to stay here. Don't be crazy.

JACK: Esther is bound to be delighted at this turn.

RUTH: Please don't bring Esther into this—

JACK: I can just see it. She'll be going around to everyone and saying "It was his fault, you know, it was *his fault.*" And I won't even be there to call her an asshole. The triumph of the utterly mediocre.

(*The phone rings. Lights change.*)

RUTH: Tell me that you'll be miserable without me. Tell me you'll be as miserable without me as I'll be without you. Tell me that you won't forget me and that you'll lie awake at night thinking about me.

(*The phone rings. Lights change back.*)

JACK: Do you want to get married, Ruth? Let's get married. What am I waiting around for? Let's marry, have a Baby Ruth, and move on.

RUTH: You don't mean that.

JACK: We have to get married to stay together? Then let's get married.

RUTH: Don't kid around, Jack, it's not funny.

JACK: I'm not kidding around. You said you wanted a husband. Here he is! Let's throw on some clothes and go buy a license. What do you say. Think there's an all-night marriage bureau open somewhere?

RUTH: But you don't believe in marriage, remember?

JACK: Of course I don't believe in marriage! I refuse to believe in marriage! But I'll marry you to keep us together. (*She says nothing.*) What's the matter? What is this? Are you turning me down?

RUTH: How can you get married if you don't believe in marriage?

JACK: Fish don't believe in water, but they swim in it. I'll be the Kierkegaard of marriage, living in an element I know to be absurd.

RUTH: I'm supposed to believe you now, after all I've heard from you about marriage for six months?

JACK: Yes, he said, yes I will he said, yes yes yes.

RUTH: I'm afraid that this is all just a little too easy.

JACK: Easy . . . ?

RUTH: You think that we could just go on as we are. But we couldn't. Some things would have to change. And you have to realize that.

JACK: Well hey, this is romantic. I thought when somebody proposed, people started screaming and crying and falling into each other's arms.

RUTH: Okay. Let's think about this in detail. If we decided to get married we'd have to agree on certain things.

JACK: All right. Like—?

RUTH: Well I'm not going to marry you if we don't have kids.

JACK: I know that. Of course I know that—

RUTH: But I don't mean in ten years, Jack. I mean soon.

JACK: What does "soon" mean?

RUTH: It means very soon.

(*Small pause.*)

JACK: Are you pregnant?

RUTH: No. (*Small pause.*) It also means that we'd have to find a place big enough for a family to live in.

JACK: But this is a very big apartment.

RUTH: Not big enough for a family. Ultimately we'd have to think about whether we wanted to live in the city at all. And schools. What kind of school, and where . . .

JACK: Hey! The kid's not even born yet!

RUTH: And what it ultimately means is that you'd have to find a different job. We can't live on six thousand dollars a year.

JACK: But I *like* my job. You know that.

RUTH: Yes I know that you like your job, but it's not what a family can live on these days. If you want to teach then maybe you can find a better school, or teach at a college. I'm sorry, but—

JACK: Who is this person I'm talking to here? Could I talk to Ruth again, please?

RUTH: You're not going to live off of me, Jack.

JACK: *Live* off of you?

RUTH: Okay, I'm sorry I said that.

JACK: LIVE OFF OF YOU?

RUTH: Well you might as well be living *here,* for one thing. The way you've settled into this apartment.

JACK: I thought you *liked* having me over here.

RUTH: Since your own apartment is too small to live in.

JACK: I have lived in that apartment for many years, thank you. And I haven't been over here for the real estate, you know.

RUTH: It's very easy to be a socialist when your girlfriend's got a nice big apartment. I buy the food, I buy the—

JACK: I chip in for food! I pay my own way!

RUTH (*slightly overlapping his last words*): I'm even the one who keeps you in liquor, since you can't afford intoxication on your own salary. Do you realize that I've even been providing the *friends* in this relationship?

JACK: And I've been providing the punch lines.

RUTH: You don't have any friends, so you just use mine.

JACK: *Use* yours?

RUTH: Yes, or however you want to—

JACK (*cutting in on her*): What, have I been getting dirty fingerprints all over your friends or something? Have I been leaving the cap off your tube of acquaintances? Okay, you have a large circle of friends and I don't. I'm happy this way. What were we supposed to do when we started going out? Exchange friends, like hostages?

RUTH: It just says something, Jack.

JACK: What.

RUTH: It says something about you, that you have no friends. About the way you live.

JACK: All right. What does it say?

RUTH: It says how isolated you are.

JACK: But there's no news here. What have you been doing going out with me for six months? If you want somebody normal, toss a brick out the window and you'll hit one.

RUTH: It says you don't try to fit in very well.

JACK: But you've known all these things about me for six months. You've known how I live and what I think. And if you knew all those things, why did you ask me to marry you in the first place?

RUTH: Because I hoped against hope you'd jump in the air and say yes, and actually make me believe you. Which you didn't. And I had my answer. I had my answer all right. Classic Jack.

JACK: Well what the fuck have you been doing with me for six months?

RUTH: Maybe I hoped you were kidding all that time. That you'd do away with marriage, and kids, and cars, and political parties—

JACK: You joined in that game, too.

RUTH: Have you ever stopped and just *listened* to yourself? And realized what an asshole you can be? You don't believe in this, you don't believe in that, no private property, no marriage, no religion, no love. Not even love?! Not even the lowest common denominator?

JACK: What do you want me to say? That I believe in love? Okay. I believe in love. Do you want me to say that I love you? I love you, Ruth. *I love you.* (*Silence.*) Are we transformed now? Are we different? Are we better than we were before?

RUTH: How can you live in the world believing in nothing? How can you get up from day to day?

JACK: I can live in the world because of people like you.

RUTH: Oh, that's very beautiful.

JACK (*over her words, slightly*): *Because of people like you.*

(*Phone rings.*)

RUTH: I won't live with you.

JACK: Do you need a contract?

RUTH: And there's one other thing.

JACK: Yes?

RUTH: If we ever got married our kids would have to be brought up Jewish. I'd never agree to marry you without that.

JACK: Which means—?

RUTH: Brought up Jewish.

JACK: They'd be Jewish anyway. Isn't that Jewish law or something? That it's passed through the mother? So what's the—?

RUTH: That's not what I mean.

JACK: You mean—?

RUTH: If I ever had kids I'd want them brought up the way I was. I wouldn't feel right if my kids didn't go to temple and Hebrew school and do *tashlich* and everything else I did.

JACK: *Hebrew school?*

RUTH: That's right.

JACK: You're kidding.

RUTH: Nope.

JACK: What for?

RUTH: To learn Hebrew.

JACK: Yeah I know but—*what for?* Are there any great detective novels written in Hebrew? Besides the Bible, I mean?

RUTH: I went to Hebrew school when I was a kid.

JACK: I toasted cats over bonfires when I was a kid, but that doesn't mean I'd want my kids to do the same.

RUTH: Your grandmother was German and you—

JACK (*underneath*): Great-grandmother.

RUTH: —and you speak German. I'm Jewish and I'd want my kids to learn Hebrew.

JACK: Do you really think that I could buy that?

RUTH: You have to buy it.

JACK: Well what are you going to do? Are you going to tell your kids that there's a god? A Jewish god?

RUTH: I don't know what I'd tell them.

JACK: An Isaac Bashevis Singer in the sky?

RUTH: I don't know what I'd tell them.

JACK: You'll have to tell them something. And don't you think you'd better think about it before you have them?

RUTH: What would you tell *your* kids?

JACK: I'd tell them I don't know. I'd tell them to think about it.

RUTH: Well I couldn't do that.

JACK: So what the fuck do you do?

RUTH: You bring them up in a tradition and let them figure it out for themselves.

JACK: Oh. A tradition.

RUTH: That's right.

JACK: Sure. So they can produce more kids like you, who just pass the shit on without thinking about it. You're a smart woman, Ruth! You're a twentieth-century adult!

RUTH: Kids can't just grow up in a void, like you did.

JACK: I did not grow up in a void.

RUTH: Kids can't just grow up with nothing.

JACK: But you don't believe any of that stuff!

RUTH: How do you know what I believe?

JACK: Do you believe it? Jewish law? Pork is dirty? Everything?

RUTH: This doesn't have to do with believing.

JACK: *Do you believe it.* (*She says nothing.*) If you don't believe it, then why bring your kids up that way? And if you do believe it, why aren't you off living in Israel?

RUTH: Maybe I'm not a very good Jew. Maybe I'm a lousy Jew. Maybe I don't keep up with things as well as I—

JACK (*overlapping her last words*): So what are you going to pass on but lousy Jewishness? And you're not a Jew anyway. You're you, remember? You're Ruth.

RUTH: I'm afraid I am a Jew.

JACK: But that's just blood!

RUTH: I'm afraid I am a Jew.

JACK: That's just chromosomes! That's not what's important!

RUTH: What *is* important?

JACK: What you *are*.

RUTH: What I *am* is a Jew, and *that's* important.

JACK (*overlapping her words*): What you *are* is important.

RUTH (*overlapping him*): Deciding what you want out of life is important. And kids are important. And living in a tradition is important. Otherwise—

JACK: You're just hanging on to a tradition for the sake of hanging on to it!

RUTH: What's it to you if I hang on to the way I was brought up?

JACK: Just for the sake of hanging on to it?

RUTH: Yes. Maybe.

JACK: In your head you're still a twelve-year-old girl going to Hebrew school and believing what your parents tell you. You're thirty-five years old and you won't think for yourself!

RUTH: Well I can't turn my back on five thousand years of human society the way you can. And I can't treat my parents like people I met on a bus, the way you can. And I can't live two thousand years in the future, in some utopia. And don't say "what century is this anyway," because I don't care. And don't go into the "religion-is-all-superstition-and-slavery" speech, because I've heard that fucking speech a hundred thousand times. And it doesn't matter what you think the world is *supposed* to be like, because it's not like that. It's not utopia and it probably never will be. It's like *this,* and we have to live with it.

JACK: And you don't even know what you believe in.

RUTH: What is it about religion that turns you into such a fucking moron?

JACK: What is it about marriage and kids that turns *you* into such a fucking moron?

RUTH: Have you ever thought that maybe it isn't even religion in general that does this to you? Have you ever thought that maybe you're just a bigot?

JACK: Oh. A bigot.

RUTH: That's the word.

JACK: An anti-Semite. Is that what you're calling me?

RUTH: Just like your lovely parents. In *their* great tradition.

JACK: Yes. Bigots because of their *politeness*.

RUTH: Has it ever struck you that—

JACK: Sure, I'm such a bigot that I've been going out with you for six months.

RUTH: When you start in on that fucking accent, and telling those fucking jokes—

JACK (*overlapping her last words*): I have heard that same accent how many times out of *your own mouth,* lady!

RUTH: But I can say those things. You can't!

JACK: Yeah? Why can you insult the Germans and the French and anybody else, but your own tribe is sacred?

RUTH (*underneath his next phrase*): Nobody ever tried to *exterminate* the Germans and the French.

JACK: What makes it sacrilege in my mouth? And what makes you so sensitive on this subject all of a sudden?

RUTH: The way that you insult Esther and her husband?

JACK: Yes. People who *deserve* to be insulted, for their small-minded greed.

RUTH: Their "greed"?

JACK: Yes, their greed.

RUTH: Maybe what you don't like about Esther is that she's Jew-ish.

JACK: What I don't like about Esther is that she is a boring *cunt*. And that she would love to pry us apart.

RUTH: Maybe you're just a bigot.

JACK: All right. We're getting down to definitions now. I'm an anti-Semitic parasite. And you, what are you. Let's see. How about something indistinguishable from your good friend Esther. You want a house, you want a husband, you want kids, you want your blue shoes—

RUTH (*underneath his next words*): Will you shut up about those fucking shoes?

JACK: You want, you want, you want. Why not just change your name to Trendstein and find yourself a sheikh?

RUTH: I don't think that I'm being unreasonable—

JACK (*underneath her next words*): Marry into a toilet-paper for-tune.

RUTH: —to ask for certain things out of a marriage.

JACK: Since you're just a fucking *Jap*.

(*Pause.*)

RUTH: Okay. I want certain things from this world. And from a marriage. If that makes me a Jap, then fine. I'm a Jap. Does that satisfy you? I want a husband and I want a house and I want some kids who can enjoy what *I* enjoyed when I was a kid, which had much to do with being Jewish. Is that being a Jap? Go ahead and call me one. I don't think that it's a crime to want a husband and a house and kids. And I don't think it's a crime not to want to be poor in this world. Life is too short for being poor. And if you won't provide those things for me then I have to find someone who will.

JACK: "Provide" for you . . .

RUTH: How long are you planning to live the life that *you* do? Without this and without that. When are you planning to grow up a little?

JACK: *I have been living the life that I want to. On principles that I believe in.*

RUTH: Well it's not the life that I want.

(*Pause.*)

JACK: So I guess we both have our answer.

(*Pause.*)

RUTH: You're always saying that what's important is likeness.

JACK: That is what's important.

RUTH: And being alike.

JACK: We *are* alike.

RUTH: Maybe we're not as alike as we thought.

JACK: But we're the *same person,* Ruth! We are the same person!

RUTH: All you ever talk about is how awful it is to wake up alongside the same body all the time. Well that applies to us too, you know. So we'd be doomed anyway. Married or not.

JACK: "Doomed"?

RUTH: Any way you cut it, we'd be waking up alongside each other every day. And you'd hate that with me just like with anybody else. And I'd wake up one morning and you wouldn't be there.

JACK: "Doomed *anyway*" . . . ?

RUTH: Sure we have fun together. Sure we laugh a lot and have a good time. Sure we fuck well together. Other people fuck well together, too, so what's so special about us?

JACK: How long have you been planning to dump me, Ruth?

RUTH: I don't believe that you would say that—

JACK (*cutting in on her*): No. How long have you been planning to get rid of me? Since before Esther's cousin's anniversary thing, or after?

RUTH: You're such an asshole.

JACK: And I thought I was so fucking smart! You didn't really *mean* it when you asked me to marry you!

RUTH: I meant it.

JACK: That was just a *show*. I see. Well you did it very well. It was very convincing.

RUTH (*under his next words*): *I meant it!*

JACK: "Will you marry me, Jack, because if you won't then we can't be together anymore." Knowing all along what the answer was likely to be. You only asked me to marry you so that I could turn you down and you could drive me out!

RUTH: All right then, leave!

JACK: Fuck you!

RUTH: Leave!

JACK: *Fucking Jap!*

RUTH: *Then leave!*

(*Pause.*)

JACK: Okay well I guess this really is it, huh. Any way I cut it I can't win here. Any way I cut it I'm *doomed*.

RUTH: Jack, if we have to end, then let's do it . . .

JACK: How. How are we supposed to do it.

RUTH: I don't know. How do two people like us come to a stop?

JACK: I'll tell you how we do it. If this is over then that means it's over, pal. Over. You know? Over? That means that after I walk out that door—as I will very shortly—then I don't want to see you, I don't want to hear from you, I don't want you to write me, or call me—I don't even want you to think about me. I don't even want you to *remember* me. You are history, pal. You are erased. You died today.

RUTH: Don't say that—

JACK: If this is over, then this is gone.

RUTH: You can't really mean that.

JACK: *You are tearing the heart right out of me!* And then you say that I don't *mean* it? Oh Jesus! Jesus . . . !

(*Long silence.*)

RUTH: So what do we do, Jack?

(*The phone rings.*)

What do we do?

(*The phone rings again.*)

JACK: No polyester.

RUTH: No parents.

(*The phone rings again.*)

How do two people like us come to a stop?

JACK: I don't know.

RUTH: Two tall, thin, funny people who are crazy about each other?

JACK: No idea.

RUTH: So what do we do, Jack?

JACK: I don't know. Maybe we could have some kind of a time-table. You know—cut down on each other the way people quit smoking.

RUTH: Instead of Smoke-Enders—

JACK: Joke-Enders.

RUTH: First one phone call a day, then a phone call every other day, then every third day—see each other a little bit less, till we're just a crack of light under the door.

JACK: And then we vanish.

RUTH: Exactly.

JACK: So much for utopia, huh. Well but what's the difference anyway, right? Let's take the long view. Does it really matter if two shmucks in some obscure corner of the universe move off in different directions? Will the cosmos tremble?

RUTH: Nope.

JACK: Not a hair. In the shadow of eternity, we're nobodies.

RUTH: Happens every day.

JACK: A million times over. So what's the big—Jesus, Ruth. I can't even look at you. (*Takes a deep breath, puts a hand over his heart.*) And where are those braille pajamas when you really need them. To tell you where you are.

RUTH: I'm sorry, Jack.

JACK: Don't be sorry.

RUTH: I'm sorry anyway. I feel sorry.

JACK: I just can't imagine it. I'm spoiled. I can't imagine life without you. I'd be a half of something.

RUTH: I'll tell you what you'd be.

JACK: What.

RUTH: You know what you'd be without me?

JACK: What.

RUTH: Ruth-less.

JACK: Ouch. Ouch.

RUTH: Sorry.

JACK: Okay. So. We invented a new genre. Screwball tragedy.

RUTH: You know, the sad thing . . . The sad thing isn't that love comes to an end. Or that people go out of your life, or die. The really sad thing about the world is that you get over it.

JACK: I won't get over it.

RUTH: And forget.

JACK: I won't forget.

RUTH: And even forget what really happened.

JACK: I won't forget.

RUTH: A year from now, we'll be ancient history.

(*The phone rings. It rings again. Lights change, and they move back onto the bed together exactly as at the start of the play. We begin to hear the Bizet in the distance. We have returned to the beginning.*)

JACK: So why look for utopia anywhere but here.

RUTH: Utopia . . .

JACK: Why look for paradise anywhere but in this bed.

RUTH: Paradise . . .

JACK: Absolutely. Two people who are alike and who like each other.

RUTH: Do you realize what the world would be like if everybody lived like this?

JACK: We'd know how to put a world together.

RUTH: How come they never asked us?

JACK: The fools.

RUTH: As usual.

JACK: It'd be utopia.

RUTH: Absolutely.

JACK: Earthly paradise.

RUTH: And will it ever stop?

JACK: Never.

RUTH: Will it ever stop?

JACK: It'd be utopia.

RUTH: Will it ever stop?

JACK: No polyester. No parents.

RUTH: Jack . . .

JACK: It's paradise.

RUTH: Will it ever stop?

(*The lights fade until there is only a crack of light under the door. And then that's gone.*)

CURTAIN

PHILIP GLASS BUYS A LOAF OF BREAD

*This play is for Jason Buzas,
Liz Larsen, Randy Danson,
Chris Wells, and Ryan Hilliard.
The sweet sound of perfection.*

Philip Glass Buys a Loaf of Bread was first presented at the Manhattan Punch Line Theatre (Steve Kaplan, artistic director) in New York City, in January 1990. It was directed by Jason McConnell Buzas; the set design was by David K. Gallo; costume design was by Sharon Lynch; lighting design was by Danianne Mizzy. The cast was as follows:

FIRST WOMAN	Liz Larsen
SECOND WOMAN	Randy Danson
PHILIP GLASS	Christopher Wells
BAKER	Ryan Hilliard

A bakery counter with a bakery case below it. Behind the glass of the bakery case, a single loaf of bread on a shelf. A large clock high up on the wall, stopped at 12:01. A sign that says NO CHANGE. *A door to the outside, with a bell over it.*

At lights up: A BAKER *is behind the counter, smiling.* PHILIP GLASS *is before the counter. Quite serious.* TWO WOMEN *are at the door of the bakery, about to go out.* THE FIRST WOMAN *is looking back at* PHILIP GLASS. *The* SECOND WOMAN *is looking away. The* BAKER *and* PHILIP GLASS *form one distinct area, the* TWO WOMEN *another, separate from them. They all remain like that, very still for a moment.*

FIRST WOMAN: Isn't that Philip Glass? (*The* SECOND WOMAN *turns and looks.*)

SECOND WOMAN: I think it is.

BAKER: Can I help you, sir?

GLASS: Yes. I need a loaf of bread, please.

BAKER: Just a moment.

FIRST WOMAN: It's time now.

SECOND WOMAN: Yes. Let's go. (*But she doesn't move.* GLASS *turns and looks at her.*)

BAKER: Do you know that woman, sir?

(*A bell rings.*)

FIRST WOMAN	SECOND WOMAN	GLASS	BAKER
Isn't that			
Isn't that			
Isn't that			
Isn't that			
	think it is		
	think it is		
	think it is		
	think it is		
			help you sir
			help you sir
			help you sir
			help you sir
		yes I need	
		yes I need	
		yes I need	
		yes I need	
isn't that	think it is	yes I need	help you sir
isn't that	think it is	yes I need	help you sir
isn't that	think it is	yes I need	help you sir
isn't that	think it is	yes I need	help you sir
Philip Glass			
	think it is		
Philip Glass			
	think it is		
			help you sir
		loaf of bread	
			help you sir
		loaf of bread	
Philip Glass	Philip Glass		
		help you sir	help you sir
think it is	think it is		
		loaf of bread	loaf of bread
think it is	think it is		

FIRST WOMAN	SECOND WOMAN	GLASS	BAKER
		help you sir	help you sir
Philip Glass	Philip Glass		
		loaf of bread	loaf of bread
		Yes I	
	think it is		
		Yes I	
	think it is		
		Yes I	
	think it is		
a			
		loaf of bread	
	think it is		
a			
		loaf of bread	
	think it is		
a			
		loaf of bread	
	think it is		
		a	
Philip Glass			
	think it is		
		a	
Philip Glass			
	think it is		
		a	
Philip Glass			
	is		
a			
		loaf of bread	
Philip Glass			
	is		
a			
		loaf of bread.	

FIRST WOMAN	SECOND WOMAN	GLASS	BAKER
	is?		
			help
	is?		
			help
Philip			
		loaf	
Philip			
		loaf	
	think		
			can
	think		
			can
Philip			
		bread	
Philip			
		bread	
Philip	Philip	Philip	Philip
can	can	can	can
think	think	think	think
bread	bread	bread	bread
Bread	Bread	Bread	Bread
help	help	help	help
Philip	Philip	Philip	Philip
think	think	think	think
Philip	Philip	Philip	Philip
need	need	need	need
bread	bread	bread	bread
loaf	loaf	loaf	loaf
		Do I need a	
loaf of bread	loaf of bread		loaf of bread
		Can I need a	
loaf of bread	loaf of bread		loaf of bread

FIRST WOMAN	SECOND WOMAN	GLASS	BAKER
		Can I *know* a	
loaf of bread	loaf of bread		loaf of bread
			I need bread
I know	I know	I know	
I know	I know	I know	
			I need bread
I know	I know	I know	
I know	I know	I know	
			I need bread
I know	I know	I know	
I know	I know	I know	
		Isn't	
		that	
		a loaf	
		of bread?	
	think		
Philip			
		need	
			help
	think		
Philip			
		need	
			help
	think		
Philip			
		need	
			help
	think		
Philip			

FIRST WOMAN	SECOND WOMAN	GLASS	BAKER
		need	
			help
y	y	y	y
y	y	y	y
e	e	e	e
s	s	s	s
s	s	s	s
s	s	s	s
p	p	p	p
l	l	l	l
e	e	e	e
a	a	a	a
s	s	s	s
e	e	e	e
	think		
Philip			
		need	
			help you sir?
	think		
Philip			
		need	
			help you sir?
	think		
Philip			
		need	
			help you sir?
b	b	b	b
r	r	r	r
e	e	e	e
a	a	a	a
d	d	d	d

FIRST WOMAN	SECOND WOMAN	GLASS	BAKER
l	l	l	l
o	o	o	o
a	a	a	a
f	f	f	f
Philip need	Philip need	Philip need	Philip need
help you sir?	help you sir?	help you sir?	help you sir?
Philip need	Philip need	Philip need	Philip need
help you sir?	help you sir?	help you sir?	help you sir?
Philip need	Philip need	Philip need	Philip need
help you sir?	help you sir?	help you sir?	help you sir?
Philip	Philip	Philip	Philip
need	need	need	need
Glass	Glass	Glass	Glass
			do you know
	Phil		
do you know			
	lip		
			do you know
	Glass		
do you know			do you know
	Phil		
do you know			do you know
	lip		
do you know			do you know
	Glass		
do you			do you
know			know
	Glass lips	Glass lips	

FIRST WOMAN	SECOND WOMAN	GLASS	BAKER
G	G	It was	G
l	l	that	l
a	a	memorable	a
s	s	evening	s
s	s	in March	s
p	p	Out	p
l	l	at the	l
e	e	end	e
a	a	of	a
s	s	the jetty	s
e	e		e
y	y	She was	y
y	y	lying there	y
e	e	in a	e
s	s	white	s
s	s	cotton	s
s	s	dress	s
l	l	And I	l
o	o	mistook her	o
a	a	for	a
f	f	a rowboat	f
			Just a moment
It's time			
		please	
	let's go		
			Just a moment
It's time			
		please	
	let's go		
			Just a moment

FIRST WOMAN	SECOND WOMAN	GLASS	BAKER
It's time			
		please	
	let's go		
			Just a moment
It's time			
		please	
	let's go		
			Just a moment
It's time now			
let's go	let's go		
			Just a moment
It's time now			
let's go	let's go		
			Just a moment
It's time now			
let's go	let's go	let's go	
			Just a moment
It's time now			
let's go	let's go	let's go	
			Just a moment
It's time now			
let's go	let's go	let's go	let's go
Go	Go	Go	Go
Go	Go	Go	Go
Go	Go	Go	Go
Go	Go	Go	Go

FIRST WOMAN	SECOND WOMAN	GLASS	BAKER
Time	Time	Time	Time
Time	Time	Time	Time
Time	Time	Time	Time
Time	Time	Time	Time
GoGoGoGo	GoGoGoGo	GoGoGoGo	GoGoGoGo
TimeTime	TimeTime	TimeTime	TimeTime
TimeTime	TimeTime	TimeTime	TimeTime
GoGoGoGo	GoGoGoGo	GoGoGoGo	GoGoGoGo
TimeTime	TimeTime	TimeTime	TimeTime
TimeTime	TimeTime	TimeTime	TimeTime
Glass	Glass		GoGoGoGo
			TimeTime
Time	Time	It was	TimeTime
		that	
Glass	Glass	memorable	GoGoGoGo
		evening	TimeTime
Time	Time	in March	TimeTime
Glass	Glass	Out at	GoGoGoGo
		the end	TimeTime
Time	Time	of the	TimeTime
		jetty	
Time			
	is		
			a moment, sir
Time			
	is		
			a moment, sir
Time			
	is		
			a moment, sir

FIRST WOMAN	SECOND WOMAN	GLASS	BAKER
Time			
	is		
		now	
Time			
	is		
		now	
Time			
	is		
		now	
Time			
	is		
		now	
Philip			
	the		
			moment, sir
Philip			
	the		
			moment, sir
Philip			
	the		
			moment, sir
Time			
	is		
		now	
Time			
	is		
		now	
Time			
	is		
		now	
Time			
	is		
		now	

FIRST WOMAN	SECOND WOMAN	GLASS	BAKER
Go	Go	Go	Go
Go	Go	Go	Go
Go	Go	Go	Go
Go	Go	Go	Go
Time	Time	Time	Time
Time	Time	Time	Time
Time	Time	Time	Time
Time	Time	Time	Time
Philip			
	is		
		a	
			moment's
	time		
Go	Go	Go	Go
Go	Go	Go	Go
Go	Go	Go	Go
Go	Go	Go	Go
Time	Time	Time	Time
Time	Time	Time	Time
Time	Time	Time	Time
Time	Time	Time	Time
Time is	Time is		
a moment, sir	a moment, sir		
			Do you know that woman?
Time is	Time is		
a moment, sir	a moment, sir		
			Do you know that woman?
	think		
Philip			

FIRST WOMAN	SECOND WOMAN	GLASS	BAKER
		I loved her once	
			Do you know that woman?
	think		
Philip			
		I loved her once	
			Do you know that woman?
	think		
Philip			
		I loved her once	
What's the matter			
	Philip		
		I loved her once	
What's the matter			
	Philip		
		I loved her once	
			Just a moment
		once	
			Just a moment
		once	
			Just a moment
		once	

FIRST WOMAN	SECOND WOMAN	GLASS	BAKER
now			
		once	
now			
		once	
now			
		once	
now			
	nothing		
matters			
		I	
now			
	nothing		
matters			
		loved	
now			
	nothing		
matters			
		her	
now			
	nothing		
matters			
		once	
			Just a moment
			sir
Philip	Philip		Philip
need a	need a		need a
		need please	
Philip	Philip		Philip
need a	need a		need a
		need please	
Philip	Philip		Philip
need a	need a		need a
		loaf of bread	

FIRST WOMAN	SECOND WOMAN	GLASS	BAKER
Philip	Philip		Philip
need a	need a		need a
		need please	
Philip	Philip		Philip
need a	need a		need a
		need please	
Philip	Philip		Philip
need a	need a		need a
loaf of love	loaf of love	loaf of love	loaf of love
What's the			
woman			
matter			
			need
		change	
What's the			
woman			
matter			
	Philip		
		go	go
		change	change
What's the			
woman			
matter			
	Philip		
		now	now
		change	change
		need	
			woman
		need	
	nothing		
		need	
matter			

FIRST WOMAN	SECOND WOMAN	GLASS	BAKER
need help	need help	need help	need help
		need woman	need woman
	need nothing	need nothing	
need matter		need matter	
so what?	so what?	so what?	so what?
lovelove	lovelove	need woman	need woman
lovelove	lovelove	know nothing	know nothing
lovelove	lovelove	need matter	need matter
need change	need change	need change	need change
lovelove	lovelove	need woman	need woman
lovelove	lovelove	know nothing	know nothing
lovelove	lovelove	need matter	need matter
	it's time	it's time	
lovelove	lovelove	need woman	need woman
lovelove	lovelove	know nothing	know nothing
lovelove	lovelove	need matter	need matter
	no love	no love	
need woman	need woman	need woman	need woman
know nothing	know nothing	know nothing	know nothing
need matter	need matter	need matter	need matter
go know	go know	go know	go know
need woman	need woman	need woman	need woman
know nothing	know nothing	know nothing	know nothing
need matter	need matter	need matter	need matter
no change!	*no change!*	*no change!*	*no change!*

(*The bell rings again.*)

BAKER: Do you know that woman, sir?

GLASS: Yes. I loved her once.

FIRST WOMAN: What's the matter?

SECOND WOMAN: Nothing. Nothing. (*The* TWO WOMEN *go out.*)

PHILIP GLASS: I also need some change.

(*The* BAKER *points to the* NO CHANGE *sign.*)

BLACKOUT

"The play's the thing..."
—*William Shakespeare*

WOODY ALLEN

Hannah and Her Sisters $10.00/0-394-74749-6
Three Films: *Zelig, Broadway Danny Rose,* $16.00/0-394-75304-6
   The Purple Rose of Cairo

ROBERT BOLT

A Man for All Seasons $8.00/0-679-72822-8

ALBERT CAMUS

Caligula and 3 Other Plays: *The Misunderstanding,* $7.96/0-394-70207-7
   State of Siege, The Just Assassins

SPALDING GRAY

Monster in a Box $9.00/0-679-73739-1
Sex and Death to the Age 14 $11.00/0-394-74257-5

JOHN GUARE

Six Degrees of Separation $10.00/0-679-73481-3
Four Baboons Adoring the Sun and Other Plays: $12.00/0-679-74510-6
   Something I'll Tell You Tuesday, The Loveliest
   Afternoon of the Year, A Day For Surprises, Muzeeka,
   In Fireworks Lie Secret Codes, The Talking Dog,
   New York Actor

LILLIAN HELLMAN

Six Plays: *The Children's Hour, Days to Come,* $13.00/0-394-74112-9
   The Little Foxes, Watch on the Rhine, Another
   Part of the Forest, The Autumn Garden

DAVID MAMET

Oleanna $10.00/0-679-74536-X

EUGENE O'NEILL

Anna Christie, The Emperor Jones, The Hairy Ape $8.00/0-394-71855-0
The Iceman Cometh $8.00/0-394-70018-X
Three Plays: *Desire Under the Elms, Strange* $8.00/0-394-70165-8
   Interlude, Mourning Becomes Electra

JEAN-PAUL SARTRE

No Exit and Three Other Plays: *The Flies,* $10.00/0-679-72516-4
   Dirty Hands, The Respectful Prostitute

SAM SHEPARD

States of Shock, Far North, and Silent Tongue $12.00/0-679-74218-2

VICTORIA SULLIVAN AND JAMES HATCH

Plays By and About Women $9.00/0-394-71896-8

J. M. SYNGE

Complete Plays $10.00/0-394-70178-X

WENDY WASSERSTEIN

The Heidi Chronicles and Other Plays: $11.00/0-679-73499-6
   Uncommon Women and Others, Isn't It Romantic

Alex- 213   818
Gideon 655   340
       6469   4661